# ANCIENT ALIEN EMPIRE

# MEGALITHIA

## By

## Rob Shelsky
## And
## George A. Kempland

Ancient Alien Empire
Megalithia

ISBN-13: 978-1492872979
ISBN-10: 1492872970
PUBLISHED BY:
GKRS PUBLICATIONS
Copyright © 2013 by Rob Shelsky and George Kempland

This is a work of nonfiction. The authors acknowledge the trademarked status and trademark owners of various products referenced in this work of nonfiction, which have been used without permission. The publication/use of these trademarks is not authorized, associated with, or sponsored by the trademark owners. All quotations and/or related materials are referenced either in the body of this book itself, or referenced at the end.

All works cited herein have their sources included. All illustrations/photos are courtesy Wikimedia Commons Public Domain images. Short portions of Public Domain documents, such as the Bible, etc., have been reproduced herein.

\* \* \* \* \*

DEDICATED
*IN MEMORIUM*

TO

# *GEORGE A. KEMPLAND*

Author, Friend, And So Very Much More
1929 — 2013
*Wherever You Are Now, George,*
*May You Always Be Happy, At Peace, And Enjoy Yourself.*
*Wherever You Are,*
*I Hope I May Get To See You Again... Somewhen.*

# Table of Contents

# Introduction

Aliens, have they visited our world now or in the past? Perhaps they came to Earth in our far past, even so long ago they might have arrived at the time when we first became a distinct species, or possibly even before that? Did an ancient empire once exist and did aliens control it? If so, what was the purpose of their Empire? Why were they here? In addition, if they were here, why does that Empire no longer exist? What happened?

Many have attempted to answer these questions. Many have devoted themselves to trying to resolve these issues. The subject of ancient aliens is of particular if not of truly singular interest to many people.

Well, we're no different. Ancient aliens concern us, as well. The idea such beings might have once visited our planet in the past seems to us a very real possibility. It is, in our opinion, even likelihood. We think there is credible evidence for this idea from a variety of sources. We think there is sound evidence of them once having dominated our world.

We are going to discuss this topic here in this book, the evidence for *Ancient Alien Empire, Megalithia*. It is our theory such an empire existed and aliens or multiple alien races controlled it. We'll explain why we think this is so, attempt to provide evidence, try to explain the workings of that Empire, its political makeup, geographical and timespan, technology, social structure, and *raison d'être,* its reason for being. We will also discuss the fall of the Empire, its immediate aftermath. We will delve deep into all the aspects of an alien empire we feel certain once existed on Earth.

However, and this is most important, something new. We are attempting to create a synthesis, an overall framework for the whole topic of ancient aliens, finally to bring it all together. Up until now, authors have focused just on various facets of the topic. We want to bring it all together, under one roof, as it were.

We feel we have done this by incorporating credible new theories, including, but not limited to, the cause of the "Big Freeze," the destruction of the mega-fauna at the end of the last Ice Age, as well as the true cause of the Great Flood. We hope to convince you of these theories. With this in mind, let us begin to find out more about that ancient alien civilization that once dominated our planet, that Empire for which we have chosen to coin the name, "Megalithia."

# PART 1

## CONTENTIONS
## AND
## A LOGICAL PREMISE FOR ALIENS

# Chapter 1

## Our Contentions Regarding Megalithia

**B**efore we even try to establish anything with the available evidence, we would like clearly to state our contentions. Here they are:

**Contention 1. We think aliens came to Earth and established an ancient civilization on this planet, a worldwide one that we've named Megalithia.** We chose the name for the megalithic stone structures that seem to have been such a hallmark of the era, been such a dominant feature of that civilization.

**Contention 2. We believe the aliens were the undisputed and absolute masters of Megalithia.** We believe and hope to demonstrate the fact the aliens utterly controlled that civilization in every sense, virtually every aspect, including economy, transportation, technology, society, government, and even the architecture and the arts. In other words, humans were subjects and slaves, and not much more. At best, perhaps humans might have been lucky enough to be considered trusted servants in some rare instances.

**Contention 3. We feel there is evidence there might have been more than one alien species involved.** As we delved deeper into this idea, we came across a number of sources of information that seem to strongly support the indication there could well have been more than one alien species visiting here, perhaps many more.

**Contention 4. There is evidence these alien species**

may all have been vying with each other for control. This control was not only of Earth, but this general region of space, as well. The same sources as we will use for our Contention Number 3, above, also suggest there was friction, strife, and ultimately a war among the alien races, and even internal divisions among members of the same species.

**Contention 5. It is our belief, backed by various forms of evidence, that a major war or civil war ensued, which also could have involved a human rebellion.** If so, this wasn't just a regional war, but rather a worldwide one, even an interstellar one, given the nature of some of the evidence we've found.

**Contention 6. In our estimation, it is almost certain the conflict had disastrous consequences for the aliens.** For them, the war may have ended an interstellar empire, or at least destroyed it in this sector of the Milky Way Galaxy.

**Contention 7. For us humans, the war had disastrous consequences, as well, and meant the utter collapse of the Megalithian civilization.** We were plunged as a species into disunity, isolation, and barbarism. The First Great Dark Age, as we call it, came upon us and with it a form of racial amnesia, a loss of memory of what had come before.

**Contention 8. Humanity, worldwide, became a retrograde culture.** With the withdrawal of our alien overlords and the ensuing chaos, our civilization collapsed. Technology, what little we humans were actually privy to, vanished without the support of the alien over-structure. (Note: We use "over-structure" here, because this term is much more appropriate for what we have in mind, rather than the more usual term, "infrastructure.")

**Contention 9. The very geography of the coastal regions of the world changed and the climate radically altered.** Based on maps, real drowned cities, and legends and myths of various cultures, as well as real archeological evidence, we believe a cataclysmic event took place that altered the coastlines of our globe. What's more, it dramatically changed the climate for the worse. We think this change even involved a new idea of ours, the creation of the "Big Freeze," otherwise known as the Younger Dryas Period." This is a new idea, and no one else has thought until now to incorporate it into an overall picture, a synthesis of all the evidence people have talked about with regard to ancient aliens up until now. We feel this theory helps tie our whole premise together.

**Contention 10. Up to several millennia would pass before we began to emerge from this primitive state of existence, the First Great Dark Age.** A long time would pass before we once more began to grow in numbers and knowledge, and thus pull ourselves up by our bootstraps, but with a difference; this time, the knowledge would be of our own making and so integral to our civilization. This time, we would create what would truly be our "own" civilization. Instead of contained in place by an over-structure imposed on us by aliens, it would be welded solidly together by infrastructures of our own devising.

Our past with the aliens would be forgotten in that long process of recovery. The Megalithian era in our human history would vanish from our collective conscious, except for lingering on in the form of legends, myths, and stories. This, we believe, humanity did—forget. If you think it should be impossible for us to forget such a past, we have examples from recent times of just such events happening. We will discuss these later on in this book, when we discuss each of these contentions in much more detail and provide evidence for them.

**Chapter Note:** If all this seems implausible to you, then please bear with us and withhold your judgment. Try to approach the topic with an open mind. In this book, we will strive to give you the evidence to support the above contentions as best we can. We will attempt to build not only a plausible, but perhaps even probable case for all this we've stated as being likely.

We intend to show evidence and not just suppositions for what we say. In so doing, we think we can make a strong case for our arguments.

Still, in the final analysis, it will be you, the readers, who must decide this for yourselves. All we can do is state our theories, provide what evidence we have for them. We hope it is enough to convince you.

**Chapter Conclusion:** We think we can convince you! Now we will proceed to try to do just that with the above list of contentions, and evidence for each of them. It's important to note these contentions form the structure, the very framework of our theory of *Ancient Alien Empire, Megalithia.*

## Chapter 2

## Simple Logic

First, why do we even think aliens were here at all, let alone once having had an empire? Well, the answer is we feel simple logic explains it, makes it highly likely, even if no other evidence existed. We'll enumerate each point of that logic here:

**1.** First, let's start with ourselves, we humans. We have constantly grown as a species. With every century, there are more of us and we have learned more. This is a simple fact. Over the millennia, our sum total of knowledge has grown to the point where it now doubles at a faster and faster rate. Multiple sources describe the growth of our knowledge as exponential in nature.[1]

Of late, the accumulation of, and the speed with which such knowledge is coming to us, has truly exploded. So incredibly quickly has this happened in the last several decades alone, some are referring to it as becoming an information implosion, or a "technological singularity."[2]

What is a technological singularity? Well, Vernor Vinge, a prominent science fiction writer invented the term. He said:

> *"We will soon create intelligences greater than our own. When this happens, human history will have reached a kind of singularity, an intellectual transition as impenetrable as the knotted space-time at the center of a*

*black hole, and the world will pass far beyond our under-standing."*

—Vernor Vinge, Author, 1983

Now unless you think he was just "another science fiction author" blowing hot air, please understand he was merely creating, as we are with this book, a synthesis of ideas and notions previously discussed by many others, including none other than the famous Alan Turing.

Turing was the man who greatly helped to break the German "Enigma Code" of World War II. He later came up with the concept of the Turing Test for artificial intelligence. It says that if in a blind test you ask both a human and a computer the same series of questions and you can't tell by the results, which one is the human, than for all practical purposes you have a true artificial intelligence.[3]

So Vinge's concept was that when we achieved a breakthrough, the "technological singularity." It is something many scientists think is almost upon us now. Then the artificial intelligence so created could then go on to create even better and more powerful versions of it. This is also referred to as the concept of "transhumanism."[4]

If you think this is an unlikely idea, please understand the concept is based on a solid foundation, one known as "Moore's Law."[5] Moore's Law describes the very real and exponential rate of growth in computer power as it is happening, today, right now. Therefore, this isn't just a fantasy, but a real fact, one that's happening even as we speak.

The idea of a "Kurzweil's Law,"[6] is a variation on Moore's Law, is also known as "the law of accelerating returns" and refers to the ability of such new artificial intelligences then being able to create better versions of themselves at the same rate as we are now improving computers.[7]

This conclusion would seem to be just simple logic, as evidenced by Kurzweil. "Ray" Kurzweil, by the way, is a futurist and author, and unless you think him unqualified to discuss this subject, we must add that he is a Director of Engineering at Google, no less.[8] In other words, the man "knows his stuff."

Now how close to the present time will this take place? Well, of course, there is a lot of controversy about this, but Kurzweil thinks we will have computers that are comparable in power to the human brain by 2020 and through the process of reverse engineering, true artificial intelligence by around 2030.

This is the singularity point for him, the beginning of the "Post-Human Age." In other words, this will occur in no more than two decades, probably, and not hundreds or even thousands of years into the future, as some would like to think and perhaps even hope. We are tottering on the brink of "transhumanism" right now, it would seem.

Why do we mention this here in a book about an ancient alien empire? What does this have to do with ancient aliens? Well, we'll get to that in just a couple of more paragraphs, but our point right now is that we have reached the stage in our civilization where we literally cannot absorb the amount of data and information we are receiving. Yet, we are using such data, even so.

Our technologies are growing at an incredible rate. Our research into everything from medicine to quantum mechanics has taken off. We're finding answers to all sorts of questions—everything from genetic manipulation of our and other species' genes, to cloning of animals, building better rocket ships, putting robots on Mars and other worlds, new drives for rockets, such as with the "ion drive," and even the first attempts at teleportation, which attempts have met with some limited success already.

An entire atom has been teleported already. This may not seem a big deal, but trust us, it is! It proves the concept of teleportation actually works, has moved the idea from the realm of science fiction to that of science fact.

All this is just a fraction of the total of what we are discovering, learning, developing, and creating. Every one of those new discoveries adds still further to our knowledge base of humanity, and so the process grows even more and ever more quickly.

Of course, in that process, we're also finding more questions. That would seem to be the norm. Even so, we are finding many answers along with those new questions, as well. Now having gotten this far, let's follow this logic trail:

**Question:** Is our knowledge base growing and will it continue to grow?

**Answer:** Yes, our knowledge is increasing at an ever more rapid rate. As stated, it is growing exponentially.[9] For instance, all of human knowledge from the beginning of civilization to 1952 was then doubled in the next fifteen years. Then it doubled again in half that time, and so on. Our sum total of knowledge takes less than 72 hours now to double, and then that will halve, and then even that will halve, *ad infinitum*, it would seem. This is what we mean by the term, "exponential growth rate." We stress this "exponential" part of it for a reason, because this is just a logical projection of a trend that has been going on for thousands of years and is going on right now.

**2. Question**: If our knowledge were growing rapidly, if our supply of information is growing exponentially, then logically, why wouldn't this also have happened to other races, other sentient beings residing elsewhere in the universe? After all, most scientists, mainstream scientists at that, now think life elsewhere, including sentient life, is more probable than not.[10] To quote one source:

*"Hence, if you believe that a typical civilization lasts 1/2 of its star's lifetime, then our Galaxy* **[alone]** *probably contains 200,000 advanced communicating civilizations (as many as 1 million), the average distance between civilizations will be roughly 250 to 400 light years, and our 50 year-old radio and TV signals may have already been picked up by the closest neighbors!"* [**Emphasis added.**]

Source: www2.astro.psu.edu/users/dfox/A001/Notes/lec37.htm

**Answer:** With the discovery of numerous, even thousands of extra-solar planets, that is, planets outside of our own solar system, this idea seems all the more likely now to be a real possibility, even probability. It is now estimated (very latest estimate as of the date of this book) that there may be as many as 200 to 500 billion stars in our Milky Way galaxy alone.[11] The number of planets is then estimated at around 100 billion in our galaxy.

This works out to about (and this is an incredibly large number) 50 sextillion planets in the universe, if not more. The number is so large it's inconceivable and it keeps growing with every new estimate.[12]

This is why most scientists think there is not only life teeming in the universe, but there must be an incredible number of intelligent species "out there," even perhaps in our own galaxy, the Milky Way.[13] Who are we to argue with scientists? Moreover, here is where logic comes into play:

**Logical Projection:** Surely, if the above information is to be believed with regard to life, and other sentient races, then even allowing for a wide variance in such scientific estimates, the logical conclusion must be that intelligence is not unique to just this one average planet—far from it. Intelligence may exist throughout the universe and may be "common."

If this is so, then this means the ability to acquire knowledge isn't just limited to us, either. It would appear likely that just as intelligence may be widespread, so, too, the accumulation of knowledge is a natural part of being intelligent and so, too, is widespread.

Therefore, if anyone exists "out there," or has ever existed "out there," then this would seem to be a very reasonable thing to conclude. It's a straightforward logical deduction.

Let's now make a logical projection based on this information:

If alien races exist or have existed in the past, then:

**(a)** They are capable of acquiring knowledge, just as we are, since this very ability is a big part of the definition of intelligence.

**(b)** If they acquire enough of it, then just as we would like to do, some of them may choose to visit worlds inside and outside of their own solar system, just as we want to do,

**(c)** This means some of them might well have developed a method of traveling the vast distances of interstellar space (as we are trying to do right now, with NASA offering a reward for this), and so have visited our planet Earth, and,

**(d)** Since some alien races must have been born long before our own species, they must be technologically well ahead of us. Remember our references to the "technological singularity?" Well, they come into play here. If we are on the verge of it right now, then by sheer logical deduction, other races must be on the brink, as well, or already have reached it, and maybe some of them did perhaps millions or even billions of years before us! This means they might well have achieved such interstellar flight abilities as much as a million, or even a billion years ago!

Does this seem farfetched? It shouldn't. Again, it's simple logic. Some of those races must have been born well before we were.

This idea is further validated by recent information that suggests "rocky worlds," such as Earth, may have developed much earlier on in the formation of the universe and its galaxies than we had previously thought, even before the gas giants could have done.[14]

This means planets with life, intelligent life, as well, could have gotten a much earlier start in the history of the universe than we once suspected. Therefore, very old alien civilizations really could be "out there."

If this is true, then they have probably developed some sort of method of interstellar travel. After all, given enough time, we will probably do the same, once our technology will allow us the capabilities of doing so. This has already partially begun. We have already touched or actually landed on our nearest neighbors, the Moon, Mars, Venus, and even a moon of Saturn, that methane-shrouded world, Titan. We even have a spacecraft, *Voyager 1* that has already left our solar system. It is in true interstellar space, now traveling through that dark void that exists between stars.

As mentioned, just recently and using the latest telescopes and sensing devices, we have turned our eyes to the stars, to search for planets around distant suns. Amazingly, we have already discovered thousands of them. So as our abilities in exploring other worlds increase, wouldn't it be logical to assume the same phenomenon would have happened for other species, intelligent creatures not of this world?

**3. Question**: Have other alien species had enough time already to do this, and so may have already come to our world?

**Answer**: The quick answer is, yes. The earth is approximately 4 ½ billion years old. As ancient as that may seem, that's still young compared to the age of the universe as a whole. The universe, or as some prefer to call it now, the multiverse, dates back the better part of 13 billion years and perhaps more. Some estimates place it at 13.82 billion years old.[15]

Consequently, it seems eminently reasonable that somewhere during that vast amount of time, other species have discovered the capabilities and means of coming here. You see, we may be newcomers on the universal scene, but that doesn't mean everyone else is, too. The universe is old enough that many intelligent species may have been born, developed, and already have died out.

In addition, that means there has been plenty of time for alien races to visit our world sometime during the past 4-1/2 billion years. Just maybe, some of them didn't leave, but decided to stay. That's our argument with this chapter. That we have been visited by aliens and some of them decided to stay on Earth and use its resources to their advantage.

**Chapter Conclusion:** So it is very reasonable, only logical, to conclude that other alien races probably exist and have existed, and some have developed enough knowledge to come here at some time in our past, perhaps even our remote past. We think, utilizing this same logic, they've had more than enough time to do this already and some have done so.

Furthermore, our world would be a special attraction to them. We intend to argue it had something they wanted in particular, besides just being a fair planet, a lovely blue marble, Earth.

We feel those who argue the technology doesn't exist to accomplish such a feat as true interstellar travel, are like babies trying to tell their parents that the world is no bigger than what they can see immediately around them. The parents, far more experienced, know better, of course.

So who are we, absolute newcomers on the galactic scene, and mere babes in the celestial woods, to say what is possible and what isn't? Maybe, with another million to billion years of civilization behind us, we might just have enough experience to know what we're talking about in this regard, but not yet.

What might more advanced technologies, ones that have had millennia or even millions of more years of existence be capable of accomplishing? One estimate says the entire galaxy could already have been explored several times over since it's been formed. That's by intelligent species that *cannot* travel faster than the speed of light! Estimates are it would take around four million years for one species alone to explore the Milky Way completely using standard, sub-light speeds.[16]

As so many infomercials say of late: "But wait! There's more! We feel there is more, as well, much more involved here.

We've just shown using simple logic and by quoting a variety of impeccable sources and reliable references that logically, it is very possible, even highly probable Earth may have already been visited by another species at some point in its 4.5 billion-year existence.

Now, having set the premise for this distinct possibility, even probability of alien visitation in our past, we'll next discuss our contention as to why we think Megalithia, that ancient alien empire, actually existed here on Earth. At this point, we now move from simple corroborating logic to actual supporting evidence for this theory and others we've developed.

# PART 2

# AN OVERVIEW OF THE MEGALITHIAN EMPIRE

# Chapter 3

## What Was the Nature of the Megalithian Empire?

**M**egalithia, that probably most ancient of all empires on Earth—did it really exist? Was there truly a world-girdling civilization, one ruled by alien masters, perhaps even more than one species of them? It sounds rather like an incredible myth, some crazy "made up" story, or some preposterous legend, doesn't it? Yet, we feel something very much approximating Megalithia did actually exist. In this chapter, we start to provide evidence for this claim.

First, what was Megalithia like? What do we know about it? Well, based on the evidence we have gathered, we feel it had certain very notable features. Following, are the hallmarks of the first great civilization on Earth:

**1.** As mentioned above, this civilization spanned the entire globe. As of yet, we have not determined when it may have arisen, and in this regard, possible start dates seem to be all "over the map." Some evidence suggests the alien civilization started as much as a quarter of a million years ago, and oddly, there is some real evidence for something like this seeming to have been possible. We simply can't argue this convincingly, though, since we don't feel there is quite enough evidence to do so.

However, we do believe Megalithia must've been at its peak at or around 8,500 to 10,000 B.C.E., approximately. In other words, it was at its zenith at about 10,500 to 12,000 years ago or thereabouts, give or take a thousand years. There might be even a wider variation in this number, because we have to rely on evidence that is hard to date. We'll explain this more fully later on.

**2.** Despite being almost worldwide, the population of humans was not large. Several estimates have it as low as just one million people total.[17] Other estimates vary, but not by a great deal. By 9,500 BCE, just five hundred years later and closer to our own time, the population is thought to have jumped to around two million.[18] Even then, although double, it still didn't come to many people on a global scale, by any means.

So unlike later empires, such as Rome, where just that one city had over one million people at its peak, and the entire Empire was teeming with citizens, Megalithia probably was more a series of small settlements, perhaps geographically, and highly isolated ones. There would have been few if any cities as we think of them today. Certainly, they weren't nearly as large as those of later civilizations were. Then, it is anther of our contentions that the aliens probably didn't want huge populations of people.

**4.** The population of aliens was not large either. This created problems with regard to controlling humanity and administering their Empire. They came up with some innovative ways to accomplish this goal of theirs, though. Again, we'll discuss these methods in more depth later on.

**5.** The civilization seems to have mainly existed in coastal areas, although there were inland settlements, as well, principally for such things as mining operations, apparently. Still, so many of the settlements were on the coasts, or along river deltas near the coasts and other low-lying areas by the sea, one might even have renamed Megalithia as the "Coastal Empire," instead.

**6.** The architecture of Megalithia was unique at the time and remains so to this very day. Certain buildings were principally composed of great stone structures. When we say great, we mean truly massive, and built to last for lifetimes and millennia. Never since that time, even with modern-day equipment, has humanity built on such a scale using solid stone. It has even been questioned if we can accomplish such feats today.

Because of this, one might almost say that by comparison

to those people, we are a retrograde culture in that respect, at least when it comes to architecture. Even with our best equipment, we simply could not move some of the stones they did, certainly not without a great deal of time, effort, and expense and a lot of such modern equipment. We think they built like this for a reason and it has to do directly with the alien overlords' needs.

We have a caveat here with regard to Point Number 6. Although many massive structures were built of stone, ones that we now refer to as "megalithic," not, all structures were built this way. Perhaps we should define here what we mean exactly by the term, "megalithic."

"Megalithic" as:

> *"Adjective (Archaeology) (1) of, relating to, or denoting prehistoric monuments made of or containing megaliths…Origin: mid-19th century, from mega- 'large' + Greek lithos 'stone' + -ic"*

And a "megalith" is defined as:

> *"mega·lith, noun \ 'me-gə-, lith\*

— The **Oxford Dictionary**

> *Definition of MEGALITH: a very large usually rough stone used in prehistoric cultures as a monument or building block"*

—**Merriam Webster Dictionary**

So when we say aliens had us build megaliths, and so had a "megalithic" culture, this is what we mean. However, as near as we can tell, there was a curious dichotomy in the two types of structures built at the time. There were those great megalithic monuments, constructed for various arcane reasons, and then there were the other structures built for use by humans them-selves, which were on a most primitive level by comparison.

One is reminded of the story of the Three Little Pigs. Some structures were of stone, while the majority was probably of stick, and/or mud and wattle, if even that. We will attempt to explain why this was so a little later on, as well, when we discuss this topic in more depth.

**7.** There was trade and some commerce between the different settlements of the Megalithian Empire. Ideas were undoubtedly exchanged. Whether this was meant to be so, or not, we can't be sure, because the alien overlords, based on other evidence we've obtained, would appear to have preferred to keep human settlements isolated from each other. Even so, there is strong evidence for crossover of ideas and abilities, such as with regard to pyramid building, other types of stone monuments, etc.

Commodities were swapped. Again, we have evidence for this, as well. Ancient coal mines in North America, equally old tin mines in England, and even the discovery of nicotine and cocaine found in samples from mummies in Egypt (source of the drugs being from the Americas) all point to the exchange of various types of commodities. Raw materials were also delivered.

However, we feel the exchange of actual trade goods was probably kept to a minimal amount. It is our belief, given evidence we will show later on with regard to this subject that most of the raw materials went to the alien overlords, and did not substantially improve the lot of the average human life, if at all.

**8.** Besides the ability to create huge monolithic structures, the inhabitants of Megalithia also were capable of doing other things well, too. Pottery, for instance, using various glazes, was of good quality. There is evidence of mining and smelting. There is also evidence for many other industries, which modern archaeologists say couldn't have occurred until many thousands of years later, well after the time of Megalithia.

**9.** The primary method, that is the best means of transportation for both types of beings, alien and human, as well as for goods, was probably mostly in the hands of the aliens. However, we think for humans, some shipping via the seas also took place. With the aliens, technologically advanced aircraft, airships of some sort, were the primary means of transportation.

The shipping on the sea was probably done with much more primitive craft created by human hands. These would be the simplest wooden ships with or without sails, and/or galley-style vessels that required rowing. Although the range of these vessels probably wasn't great, we think there was a sort of "relay" system, where one people passed goods on from their ship to a ship belonging to another group of people. This way, some goods (such as nicotine, cocaine, etc.) made their way farther around the world than otherwise might have been possible.

**10.** The government of Megalithia was likely controlled directly from the highest levels. This control would be by the alien masters themselves, the ultimate overlords of Megalithia. However, we feel the aliens had a buffer between them and the rest of humanity.

To help keep themselves isolated from us humans, and to keep information about them from leaking out overly much, the aliens used an intermediary class of human government bureaucrats. Probably, this was accomplished by their first tier of servants, a priesthood, which served them directly. Appointed human kings and princes/governors, might have served, as well.

This overall government would have been in the form of a dictatorship, an absolute one. The apex of this dictatorship was the aliens, but the humans ruling in their name would have been just about as powerful, and probably just as arbitrary and autocratic. No doubt, they only answered to the priesthood and their alien masters, of course.

**11.** The industry of Megalithia would have been principally mining. In fact, it is because of mining that Megalithia probably existed. It is our contention the aliens operated under a sort of mercantile system. We use the first definition of mercantilism, which is:

> *"1. The theory and system of political economy prevailing in Europe after the decline of feudalism, based on national policies of accumulating bullion, establishing colonies and a merchant marine, and developing industry and mining to attain a favorable balance of trade."*

**—American Heritage English Dictionary**

In addition, this definition:

> *"1. Also called mercantile system economics a theory prevalent in Europe during the 17th and 18th centuries asserting that the wealth of a nation depends on its possession of precious metals and therefore that the government of a nation must maximize the foreign trade surplus, and foster national commercial interests, a merchant marine, the establishment of colonies, etc."*

**—Collins English Dictionary**

In this case, it was where the colonies, meaning Earth in this instance, existed for the good of the mother country (home world of the aliens), and the benefit of the alien races. This benefit would've been in the form of precious metals, principally gold, but possibly iron, copper, tin, and other metals, as well. The reason we used definitions for mercantilism from two different dictionaries is to illustrate an important point; most definitions of mercantilism emphasize *mining*. We contend that is principally what the aliens were here on Earth for—mining.

There would also have been some agriculture, possibly including a limited amount of animal husbandry. This would have been to supply the alien masters with foodstuffs, and the human population, as well.

**12.** Megalithian society would've been highly stratified. It would have been in caste-like, distinct layers of importance. The alien race or races would've existed at the top of the social pyramid, forming the very peak of that society, not just as the rulers, but as the ultimate aristocracy, as well. They would have wrapped themselves in mystery. They used their priesthood as a buffer. We think that so enamored were many humans of these lofty creatures, they often practiced certain means of making themselves resemble the aliens, at least, superficially. Again, we will have more on this later.

Directly under the aliens in the social hierarchy would've been their human servants, people we would now call priests. The aliens would have lived in sumptuous and spacious quarters, veritable palaces, much as British Colonial rulers did in India.

The human priests or priesthood would have literally served in the temples/palaces of their alien masters, and specifically, served them their meals, helped them to bathe, clean their quarters, wait on them, and whatever else may have been required of them. They would have been the household staff, the messengers, etc.

Because this was the most trusted position aliens could bestow, the priests, or "servants of the temple" (meaning a palace of the divine—as in the aliens being gods?) would've been held the penultimate honor, second only to the aliens themselves, with regard to the rest of Megalithian society. Of humans, they would be the most privileged ones. They would be rewarded for their loyalty, devotion, and services. They would demonstrate power over their fellow humans for this reason.

They would do this just as various priesthoods down through society have, even wielding considerable power over kings and queens, as the popes of the Catholic Church did over European rulers of the Middle Ages. Or as the Egyptian priesthood exercised power over some pharaohs—well, the list is a long one really. It includes ancient Romans, Greeks, Babylonians, Phoenicians, Carthaginians, and so many others.

As strange as this may sound, there is a correlation to this in much more modern times. That correlation is in, of all places, America. In the antebellum South of the United States, household slaves were considered to hold much better positions, far superior ones, than their field hand counterparts did. In addition, household slaves were accorded more privileges and responsibilities commensurate with the greater trust placed in them.

The term, "common field hand," is no accident. Generally, field hands were looked down upon during that period of American history, as somehow being "beneath" others of their own race, because of the type of work they performed. Although all were slaves, there definitely was a major class distinction between those in the fields, and those in the "house."

Perhaps close to being on a parity with the priesthood in Megalithia, but not quite, would have been the human kings/princes, and/or governors who were appointed on behalf of the aliens, either directly or through the human priesthood that served them. We think that for the most part, they probably did have their orders relayed to them from the aliens via the priesthood. These priests acted as intermediaries, and even interceders on behalf of their alien masters.

This was a deliberate ploy on the part of the aliens. By maintaining a distance, they maintained a special cachet, a certain type of "otherworldliness," literally. They were as gods to humans. Keeping their distance, shrouding themselves in relative secrecy, and maintaining their human priesthood servants as a buffer, all helped to keep this awe of them by humans.

Detractors might say that with such human servants, how could they keep this mystique going? Well, we have to remember that as with most priesthoods even to this very day, members are made to swear oaths of loyalty and often secrecy. There also often are now, and have been throughout history, "secret rites," ones that members of the public aren't allowed to witness or know. Almost every religion has had some form of this, the "inner mysteries" of the temple, the "holy of holies," etc.

This ensured the aliens' human priesthood was not only sworn to secrecy by such methods, but this kept the mystique going, kept the rest of the human populace in wonder of the aliens. The priesthood had a stake in this particular game, because they basked in reflected glory. Certainly, this was just one more enticement and inducement to want to hold such a position with the aliens and to help maintain the aura of mystery that surrounded them.

Furthermore, this was a strong reason for the priesthood members not to divulge their secrets. It was because of not only their sacred oaths, but also the power and prestige that resulted from their exalted positions. In other words, this was a great system created by the aliens to maintain their power. It was self-sustaining, an incredibly stable and long-lasting way to maintain the status quo.

Does this sound like an unlikely scenario? Well, let's look at a modern-day example of when such a system does break down. Let's consider the fact that today, in Great Britain, many people lament how the royal family of the United Kingdom is no longer "off limits" to the media, and that as a result they have lost their mystique, made to seem less as the exalted and "beneficent monarchs" and more as just fallible people.

Then the question immediately follows, why should an ordinary family have such power, pomp, and wealth, if they are no better, in no way different from anyone else in England? You see? Make the mysterious ordinary and immediately there is a question of their right to rule.

Where once British monarchs were considered unassailable, because they were "anointed by God," as in Shakespeare's, *Hamlet*—*"there's such divinity that doth hedge a king…"* and monarchs were even capable of curing certain types of illness if they touched a common person who had the disease, they became just ordinary.

They had become a rather dysfunctional family to many. Because of this, they have lost much of their mystique as being special and so many, although not the majority in England, now consider them underserving of their position, influence, and power in English society. Some English would like to see the monarchy, and indeed, even the entire aristocracy abolished, just as happened in America because of the Revolutionary War.

As a result, that ancient family is now in some, if still small amount of jeopardy, as to whether it will even continue to exist as a monarchy. See any parallels here with the ancient aliens and why they functioned the way they did, why they went to such pains to maintain themselves as a powerful and enigmatic presence?

Beneath these kings/princes/governors, would have been the human soldier class. Beneath these, would have been the merchants, artisans, craftsmen, shipbuilders, and sailors, such as there were. They would be the next lower rung on the ladder; those who had some skills that helped maintain the Empire of Megalithia so that humanity could do the aliens' bidding.

At the bottom rung of the social ladder would have been those who worked the mines, those in agriculture, etc. These were the common laborers. Since they were unskilled and could be easily conscripted to do such work, these people were undoubtedly held of little value in Megalithia.

There may have been an even lower slave class that did much of this work, but this we simply don't know. In any event, all humans were, in a very real way, slaves of their alien overlords, but to just lesser or greater extents.

**13.** Some other aspects of Megalithia that aren't so clear to us, but these are incredibly intriguing. Megalithia may have been a very different civilization in many ways from any we know today. We mean besides having aliens as rulers. However, these differences are, undoubtedly, also directly because of the alien influence and very much concern Megalithia's technology.

There is the matter of ley lines, for example. We simply can't be sure what their purpose was, what they were used for. Some argue that they don't even exist. Others say ley lines were following lines of magnetic force or some other type of energy in the Earth, as yet still unknown to us, but inherent in the planet. This, the aliens somehow managed to utilize is how the argument for ley lines goes.

We simply don't know for sure. If aliens were to tap into some type of energy, we have no idea what energy that would be; if such an unknown force even exists. Nonetheless, there does seem to be evidence for the existence of ley lines. In addition, where there are ley lines, there must have been some sort of a reason for them.

Moreover, the evidence for them is strong. For instance, one of the ley lines seems to run on a diagonal from Great Britain down through a portion of France and then into Italy and beyond. Scattered along this line, there are a series of towns and villages. These seem utterly disconnected from each other in every respect. They are in different countries, regions, completely different cultures, with difference languages, and social identities.

Yet, they do have one thing in common. The ancient root word for their names, regardless of the language the names of the towns are now in, all come from the word "star."[19] This simply can't be a coincidence. Yes, one or two towns that had this commonality might be merely coincidence. However, there are far too many towns and villages with this attribute for this to be so. These names are truly ancient ones, often derived from even earlier tongues.

So is this just a synchronicity, albeit an incredible one, perhaps? No, we don't think it's even that. We think all these towns were deliberately named this way, so that we would remember, or someone else would, that the ley line was there, and by someone else, we mean aliens.

It doesn't stop there. There also are forts and citadels lined up in Scandinavia along what would seem to be another ley line. The stone structures seem to have been deliberately constructed for some special reason. Why this is, again, we don't know, but it is intriguing that it should be. Then there are the major monuments of the world, which all seem to be at the same latitude.

Another intriguing, and rather curious phenomenon is how many of the megalithic structures of the time somehow seem to have something to do with the constellation of Orion. There is evidence that when some of the structures were built, they aligned precisely with Orion, and that alignment was at its best some 10,000 or more years ago.

This all adds credence to our idea that Megalithia was at its peak at around 10,000 to 12,000 years ago. Although why the constellation of Orion should be such a prominent and repeating theme in the architecture of Megalithia, escapes us. We can only make conjectures, and these we will do later on, as well as discussing each of these topics in more depth.

**14.** There is even more to Megalithia. There is some evidence that gives credence to the idea of genetic manipulation of humans and perhaps animals and humans together. Again, we will discuss this in more depth later on.

**15.** As stratified a society and inflexible a one as Megalithia seemed to possess, it also seems to have had some severe problems. Some of these originated from "out there." Others arose from here on Earth. It would seem the alien race or races, were not monolithic amongst themselves, even if they were toward us humans.

There are indications they quarreled and even fought amongst themselves. They often were at odds with each other. Remember, Earth may not have been a colony of just one race, but of a number of them. There was conflict. Whether this was between our one set of overlords and others that wanted Earth's riches, or conflicts amongst our overlords themselves, isn't clear.

Still, divisions there would seem to have been. Moreover, they, meaning the aliens, would seem to have had trouble with their subjects, their human ones, too. There is evidence there may have been rebellions, and ultimately even a possibly successful one.

Whether this rebellion resulted in the collapse of Megalithia as an empire, or whether it was a war amongst the aliens themselves, a civil war of some type, or a combination of both, which allowed this rebellion, we can't be certain. However, we do have some tantalizing clues.

**16.** We do know this; Megalithia went down with a huge crash. Almost overnight, it ceased to be. The alien masters withdrew from Earth, at least in the numbers they had been in up until then. This was after some type of major war or conflagration ensued.

Not only Megalithia, but also humanity and Earth were devastated in the process. There is evidence of a worldwide thermonuclear war. Stone structures ceased, as if overnight, to be built. There is evidence this war also took place in space, simultaneously, and one story even involves the Moon!

**17.** We make another bold contention. It is our own unique theory that this war may well have resulted in the Great Flood, and then caused another onset of cold, the "Little Ice Age," of the Younger Dryas,[20] as it is known. This, we think, was actually a nuclear winter of some sort.

We also contend this further acted to destroy what little might have been left of Megalithia by this point. Furthermore, this war wiped out the mega-fauna of the times, the mammoths, saber-toothed tigers, giant sloths, giant beavers, and other such creatures.

The Great Flood caused coastal regions around the world to drown. The settlements and towns of the times, the ones that existed along these coastal areas, flooded. Subsequently, some were permanently submerged.

Since Megalithia was primarily composed of such coastal settlements, this dealt it a deathblow from which it could not recover. Combined with nuclear attacks on various fortresses and other cities of the Empire, on the Indian subcontinent, Europe, and elsewhere, there was no way Megalithia would endure.

Most, if not all of those who controlled and governed the Empire, those who supplied it with their own technology, but under a strict leash, vanished into the dark of the interstellar night, the depths of space. Now with the aliens in flight from Earth, and Megalithia headless for lack of its overlords' presence, chaos ensued. Weather took a decided turn for the worse. Consequently, Megalithia was utterly doomed.

**18.** The First Great Dark Age and Retrograde Cultures. Another contention of ours that, as with the fall of Rome so many thousands of years later, the world quickly descended into savagery, although in the case of Megalithia, it was almost overnight. The First Great Dark Age, as we call it, descended on the world.

A hallmark of this happening was the ability to build megalithic structures, which probably was done in coordination with the aliens themselves, using their technology, simply disappeared. Even the knowledge of how to build them vanished. To this day, we puzzle over how some of it was done, how it was even possible.

No more such massive structures as the "platforms" (see below) are built after this time. Artisanship suffered. For instance, it has been found that in the earliest layers of the city of Mohenjo-Daro, the quality of the glaze on pottery was quite good. However, in successive layers higher up, and so closer to our own time, this was no longer so.

The pottery, instead of improving over time, as it should as a population acquired more knowledge of how to do such things through trial and error, instead reversed, became more primitive in execution and style, and became more primitive in nature and construct. Without the transportation provided by the aliens, humanity became pedestrian again. What few settlements of Megalithia had survived now became even more isolated.

Without the interconnection of other settlements, knowledge was lost. What rudimentary technology humans may have still possessed at the beginning of the fall of Megalithia, dwindled quickly away, as the cultures became retrograde.

If this last sounds hard to believe, consider the following: the Romans occupied Britain for well over two centuries. They built Hadrian's Wall. They built temples. They created Roman baths, such as in the city of "Bath." They built cities, as well. Among these was Londinium, now known as modern-day London, but there were many others[21].

They paved roads across the length and breadth of England, and some of the British highways existing today are still using those foundations.[22] They founded mining operations. They gave the British their laws, government, and other such cultural gifts.

Yet, despite all this, within just one to two generations of them having withdrawn from England, the British had largely forgotten they were ever there. In that short a time, it was as if the Romans, who'd given them a lasting civilization for centuries, had simply never existed in the first place, and this despite all those ruins still standing around them.

Structures such as the Roman wall of Hadrian were thought to have been built by a vanished race of unknown giants. Among the general populace, all racial memory of the Romans had gone, and almost unbelievably quickly![23]

So yes, these things happen. We believe such racial memory loss, such racial amnesia, also happened with regard to Megalithia and on even a greater scale. Nevertheless, it doesn't mean there isn't a record of that once great empire. Not only do we live amongst its ruins, but also to this day, there are numerous legends of drowned cities. Atlantis is but one of these. There are so many more.

**Chapter Conclusion:** The purpose of this chapter was not about going into great depth on these topics. Nor was it to provide evidence for them here. Instead, this chapter was just to give you an overview of what Megalithia might have been like when it was at its peak, what we believe were its main characteristics.

We have attempted here to give you some general idea of what kind of civilization it was, how it was ruled and by whom, the makeup of its society, and how it functioned economically and technologically. We also wanted you to see what kind of an empire it was, how it differed from later ones.

We also wanted to give you some idea of how the Empire may have ended. Finally, we touched on some of the more exotic aspects of the civilization, the technology. For instance. It may be that Megalithia was like no other civilization before or since that time.

Again, remember there is the matter of ley lines, of towns and villages with the root word "star" in their names. There is also the matter of why some megalithic structures run in straight lines, and along so-called ley lines. There is also the same question about fortresses and citadels that did the same thing. Therefore, we don't think Megalithia was like any other civilization we've known here on Earth. Then, its origins weren't here on our world, but "out there," instead.

We feel Megalithia was a forerunner empire to any real human one. In addition, it was alien in many ways to us, and not just because aliens ruled. We contemplate that some aspects of it may have been based on a different and perhaps deeper meaning of the knowledge of physics and the universe. If this is so, then this is knowledge we apparently haven't yet attained, or if we ever had it, have lost it.

Such knowledge is what could have made Megalithia so fundamentally different from our civilization today. Not only did that Empire have different priorities, a strange social structure, and arcane knowledge, but also its purpose was not what governments are created for today. Ruling humanity, governing us, was purely incidental. Megalithia existed solely for the benefit of the aliens. In addition, when they went away, so did that Empire.

Now that we've given you this brief overview, we'd like to discuss the various aspects of Megalithia as noted above, all we have touched on here now, but in much more detail. Now we wish to provide you with evidence that supports all of our beliefs and contentions about this now-vanished empire.

# Chapter 4

## The Age and Timespan of Megalithia

To begin at the beginning is the best way to start with our evidence. So first, we wish to establish the age or timespan of the Empire of Megalithia. To do this, we need some "hard" evidence that might tell us this. That is exactly what we have, literally, "hard" evidence in the form of stone.

You see, one of the true hallmarks of Megalithia, perhaps its single greatest and most perplexing achievement, or at least its longest lasting one, was in the form of its massive stone structures. Archaeologists of today are at a loss as to how to explain them. Their attempts to date them have produced only mixed results.

Hewn from rock, many ancient structures simply can't be reliably dated accurately. Oh, one can date the age of the stone itself, but that doesn't give the age of the structure. Instead, archaeologists must rely upon other finds in the immediate area to try to guess when such buildings might have been erected.

They also use timelines. That is, they draw upon what they already "think" they know about human history, and make sometimes rather major assumptions based on that supposed knowledge. Sometimes, this works. Sometimes, it doesn't and this results often in major controversies. This is not always the most reliable of methods of dating something by any means. Even amongst mainstream archaeologists, themselves, there is constant argument over the age of various items.

For instance, since archaeologists don't believe civilization started until after the latest retreat of the last Ice Age, then everything we find with regard to evidence for civilization must be dated (according to their theory) after that point in time, the end of the last major glacial period of the Ice Age, rightly or wrongly. This must be so in order for their beliefs to be correct. That means anything found that contradicts this premise is either:

**(1)** Incorrect,

**(2)** A hoax, or

**(3)** An "anomaly."

Yes, it is hard to date rock. That is, it's hard to date when a stone became part of a structure. Taking a chip of rock and testing it, will certainly give you the age of the rock itself, if the right conditions are present, but not the age of the thing constructed from it. Because of this, many megalithic structures date, variously, from as little as 2,000 years ago, to 9,000, to 10,000 years ago and sometimes much more.

This is one heck of a span of time. However, when you have no precise means of dating something, you will often get these sorts of variable results. So again, dating stone constructions is a difficult business at best, because of this.

Then, there are also grounds for legitimate confusion at times, as well. Undoubtedly, there have been those cultures that try to imitate older ones. They wanted to emulate their architectural ancestors, so to speak, and for whatever reasons. We've done this sort of thing ourselves.

Anyone who goes to Washington D.C. for the first time, when viewing all our monuments and government buildings such as the Supreme Court, Jefferson's Memorial, the Lincoln Memorial, and even the Washington Monument, might well be excused for thinking how like ancient Rome it all looks. This is because at the time these buildings were constructed, the style of "Neoclassic" architecture was popular. Neoclassicism was the revival of classic architecture and in this case, we mean the ancient Roman/Pan Hellenic architecture of more than 2,000 years ago.

If a thousand years from now someone were to dig in the ruins of Washington D.C. (assuming some disaster had struck it before then and caused it to be buried), and so found these structures, without knowing anything else about them, these future archaeologists might well think they had been built during the time of ancient Rome.

The only way they would know differently is by what they found around the ruined buildings in the way of our more modern artifacts. This, and perhaps some of the materials used in the erection of these monuments, would be how they'd have to go about dating the ruins. In addition, they might be wrong in the dates they chose. So cultures, such as our own, have produced similar structures to more ancient cultures, if not always on so grandiose a scale (although, sometimes they are).

This, then, can cause confusion when trying to date megalithic stone structures, as well, just as it might with those fictional archaeologists in our own future Washington D.C. Therefore, we have the problem of erroneous dating as a factor in setting the age of some megalithic structures. Some other monuments found around the world are true "anomalies," as archaeologists call them. This is a term they like to use, "anomalies," when nothing else works, no other explanations can be found, and when such structures are sitting there, staring them in the face, and are too huge to be ignored or explained away as simple hoaxes.

Actually, if you think about it, "anomaly," doesn't explain anything. It's rather similar to physicists calling the invisible stuff that helps galaxies stay together "Dark Matter." That term doesn't tell us what "Dark Matter" is at all. Neither does the term, "anomaly," tell us anything.

However, the age of some megalithic structures does seem to be fairly well established, despite these problems. These particular edifices would appear to date back to the time of Megalithia, almost assuredly.

We will cite evidence now to support our contention this is so, by giving you a number of examples. We will use these not only to describe just how massive these megalithic stones are, but also to show just how far back in time they were built, and just how hard it was to build them, especially, at a time so long ago. These are ones that even most archaeologists believe are of such an incredible age. Let's start with some of the truly inconceivable ones first:

# PART 3
# EVIDENCE FOR THE EMPIRE
# OF MEGALITHIA

# Chapter 5

## An Age Of Stone—Hard Evidence

Some questions are natural with regard to those most prominent hallmarks of the Empire of Megalithia's architecture. There are a number of mysteries surrounding them. These include, but are not limited to:

**1.** Why did they choose to use stone to so great an extent?

**2.** What were the true purposes of many of their structures?

**3.** Why did they build on such an incredibly massive scale?

**4.** How exactly did they build some of those giant stone edifices?

**5.** Why did they build such huge structures?

To find the answers to these questions, let's have a look at some of what the Megalithians left behind in the way of architecture.

# THE GREAT PLATFORMS OF THE WORLD

**The Temple of Baalbek**: This structure is without a doubt one of the most fantastic in the world. It is a huge platform, a truly massive stone foundation that makes all others pale (with few exceptions) into insignificance. Baalbek, Heliopolis, is in Lebanon. There, on an incredible stone foundation, the Romans built a temple to Jupiter.

As a strange aside, no Roman Emperor ever tried to take credit for building the massive foundation for the temple, the platform. This is odd, when you consider that emperors did not lack in hubris, and they gladly and often claimed credit for things they did not do. If the emperors of Rome had one commonality, this was it, laying claim to the achievements of others. Then, being absolute rulers, who was to stop them? Even so, no emperor every tried to take credit for the Baalbek platform.

Oddly, it was as if this one particular assertion was off limits even to those mighty rulers of the known world. Was it because Baalbek was considered such a holy site and for so very long a time before even the Romans came along that they just didn't dare? Were they, the mighty emperors of Rome, even afraid themselves of the consequences of trying to do such a thing?

Before Rome claimed it as a site for its own empire, the Greeks had it. The Romans merely copied what the Greeks had already done centuries before them. For instance, when General Pompey of Rome made sacrifice there in Baalbek in Sixty B.C.E., he was only imitating Alexander the Great, who had done the same to the God, Zeus, and many centuries before Pompey was even born.[24]

Why would the Greeks go there? Well, because even back then, it was already considered such a sacred site, and was so even before they had ever arrived, a long time before them. The Babylonians and Phoenicians thought this same thing before the Greeks.

So before all those conquerors and emperors came marching along, overrunning the landscape with their armies of the day, only to leave again like some repeating strange human tide ebbing and flowing, the monarch of Uruk, Gilgamesh, who lived sometime around 2900 B.C.E. supposedly attended the site. It was said he wanted immortality and hoped the gods could give it to him there.[25] This is based on the Epic of Gilgamesh, one of the oldest, if not the oldest epic ever written.

However, the Romans do claim credit for the building of the temple to Jupiter, as well as that of Bacchus. This, they accomplished somewhere around 27 B.C.E. However, the foundations upon which those temples stand, those that form the platform, are considered far older by everyone. Some researchers have dated the platform as far back as 9,000 years ago, or even as far back as 12,500, depending as to which source you wish to give credence. This last date puts it right in the High Age of Megalithia. Moreover, it puts it well into the last glacial period of the Ice Age.

Yes, as you might have surmised by now, the stones forming the foundation are big ones. However, to conceive of just how big they are, truly stretches the limits of one's imagination and credulity. When we say the foundation stones are large, we mean impossibly huge and we're not exaggerating. They are, in fact, the largest such stones in the world!

For example, the Trilithon,[26] which acts as the western edge or wall of the base of the temple to Jupiter, is comprised of three massive stones. Each one is a 1,000-ton block of limestone. One thousand tons! No equipment we have today is capable of lifting such an enormous rock. In fact, even with a combination of our biggest machines to do it, this is still well beyond our capacity.

Could we do it? Yes, it's theoretically possible, but it would take a great deal of effort and would be a major engineering feat, probably one of the biggest in modern times. You see, we couldn't position enough machinery around it, couldn't cram them all in close enough to have them available to lift one of those stones. We'd have to come up with some other means.

So if we would have to go to such great lengths, endeavor so hard to achieve such a thing with the mechanized technology we have today, how then was it accomplished 12,500 years ago by people we now regard as having been little more than Stone Age savages? According to one source,[27] it would've taken 40,000 men to move just one of the rocks.

When Athens was at its height in ancient Greece, a number of millennia later, it was thought to have a population around 50,000. So how was such a tremendous task accomplished so very long ago, when we had a much smaller world population, and they were supposedly just emerging from the last glacial period of the Ice Age, or even still in it? Remember, the ice didn't retreat from the northern continents until just about 10,000 years ago. Moreover, the stones may well have been placed at Baalbek 12,500 years ago!

There's more. At the quarry where they hewed the limestone blocks, there is a 1,200-ton stone, referred to as the Pregnant Woman, still sitting there. One thousand two hundred tons; how could such a thing be moved by anyone, even today? The sheer logistics of such a thing boggles the mind.

Yet at the height of Megalithia, someone, somehow, was moving 1,000-ton stones around and we're guessing they didn't use 40,000 people to do it, either. Where would they get so many people in any case? The very idea seems ludicrous to us.

After all, the entire world population, as recently as 10,000 years ago, is estimated to have been only about one million total. [28] These people were scattered worldwide, everywhere, supposedly living in small, nomadic, hunter/gatherer groups of as little as five or six people!

They supposedly did not, according to historians, gather in communities, because they weren't an agrarian-based culture. There was no need to stay in one place, if one didn't grow things. They were hardly all living in Baalbek at the time. In addition, 12,500 years ago, hunter-gatherers weren't even nearly that large in numbers in any given region. There wouldn't have been enough game to support so many people.

Nonetheless, someone was building these massive platforms. For whom and for what purpose were such amazingly large platforms constructed? Temples hardly needed such incredibly huge foundations to support them, not even close. They were of a great area, large enough to build multiple temples and structures upon, as with Baalbek.

What possible use could a vast level platform, built of incredibly big stones have for primitive peoples of such ancient times? Why expend the inconceivable amount of labor and effort, not to mention capital expense to their civilization (such as it was), to construct such things? After all, a stone platform won't feed their children, clothe them, or protect them from the elements or hostile neighbors. So what was their purpose?

There is another interesting side note here. In that most ancient of tales, The Epic of Gilgamesh, Baalbek is referred to as "The Landing Place." Landing Place? What could possibly have landed there? No vessels of the sea or river watercraft of any sort could get anywhere near there, nor could they remain upright out of water if they could. As if this weren't enough to give away the purpose of such a large platform, in the same epic there is a description of how Gilgamesh watched a rocket launch. Yes, you read right, a rocket launch. In an epic saga written thousands of years ago, there is a very clear description of a rocket launch from the platform at Baalbek.

Furthermore, it must be noted that the platform of Baalbek comprised, and still comprises, five million square feet![29] Why else would someone need such a vast expanse of leveled stone? No city was built upon it, we know that much.

Moreover, this wasn't just in Baalbek these platforms were built. Not too far away as the crow flies, was another one. It seems that for some reason, the Middle East was a hotbed for such platforms.

It should be also noted that archaeologists have long said that the Middle East was the cradle of modern civilization. A strange coincidence, isn't it? Noted author, Zecharia Sitchin,[30] believes it was the so-called gods, the Anunnaki who had these platforms constructed. He may well be right. We think he probably is. Let's move on to our next piece of evidence, as intriguing as the "Landing Place" at Baalbek has been.

**Attribution: צ.אסף from he**

**The Dome of the Rock:** Here we have another fantastic example of a very ancient and giant platform. It is incredibly similar to the one in Baalbek, Lebanon, but this one is in Jerusalem, Israel. Considered a holy place by Muslims (there is now a wonderful mosque there, which is called the Dome of the Rock), as well as considered holy by Christians, and Jews, the structures that have been built there throughout the successive centuries have all been created on a much older foundation or platform, just as in Baalbek.

Comparable in area to the Temple of Baalbek, no one can quite understand why such an incredibly gigantic foundation was ever needed, or what purpose it might have served so far back in time. Certainly, the structures that have been built on top of the platform never required anywhere near such an implausibly huge foundation to support them. Again, this is the exact same problem we have about Baalbek. What was it for?

In addition, just as with Baalbek, this site is considered very holy, and has been for a very, very long time, and by all the above-named religions. Wars have raged to control not only Jerusalem, but this "platform." It would appear there are good reasons for this. All those religions claim something special; something of a supernatural or transcendental nature took place there. The same holds true for Baalbek. It was, after all, a place considered especially holy and so dedicated to the gods by the Romans, and to the mightiest god of them all, Jupiter, and Zeus by Alexander the Great, not to mention where ancient Gilgamesh could go to obtain immortality.

For Christians and Jews, who both believe in the Old Testament of the Bible, the Dome of the Rock area was supposed to have been the site of Abraham's attempted sacrificing of Isaac, his son.[31] Only at the last minute, as the scripture goes, did God, himself, supposedly intervene to spare the boy and stay Abraham's hand. As with so many things we talk about here, it doesn't stop there!

Most archaeologists, and those who follow Jewish tradition, say the original Temple of the Mount, built by Solomon had the Holy of Holies[32] on the exact spot that is now the most revered location in the center of the mosque of the Dome of the Rock. This spot is said to be where the Prophet Mohammed ascended to heaven.[33]

Just another strange coincidence? Two different religions, and the exact same place is considered especially holy by each of them, although for different reasons, different events that happened thousands of years apart. If just coincidences, they are coming thick and fast at this point, aren't they?

In Jerusalem, that particular spot is an example of both an ancient place and a sacred place, and a place that was sacred since time immemorial, and remains sacred to this day. The fact people seem to come and go from heaven there, that God spoke from on high there, and that the original Temple[34] was supposed to have been built with the help of demons[35] controlled by King Solomon, all seems highly suggestive. Another platform, and somehow gods, or God, seem to be involved, strange legends are involved, weird claims are made, and repeatedly so over many thousands of years. This is bizarre, to say the least.

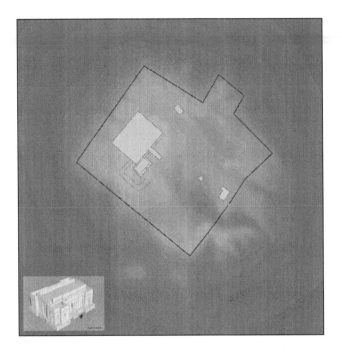

**Eridu, or E-RI-DU:**[36] The name is believed to translate to "Home Built Far Away" or as another translation puts it, "Home in the Far Away Built." Intriguing name for one of the first cities of humankind, if not *the* first, isn't it?[37]

"Far away" from where, exactly, would that be? And the fact it was also situated at the confluence of the Tigris and Euphrates Rivers, almost exactly where many historians think the original Garden of Eden had to have been located (if it existed at all), is also coincidental. One thing of note: at the time Eridu was built, the two rivers had not silted up the area as it is today. Eridu was on the coast.

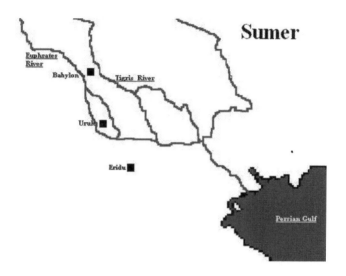

This silting process is a common occurrence, given enough time. Many Roman ports, as well as Greek, and Phoenician, had the same problems over time. Places that were once harbor towns are today miles inland.

Nevertheless, why such a name as "Eridu," a "home built faraway?" When, in fact, Sumerian legend (or as they thought of it, their actual recorded history) says it was *the* first city. Eridu is situated in the southern area of that ancient land called Mesopotamia. The modern name for it is Tell Abu Shahrain.

At the time of its first habitation, as mentioned above, a tributary of the Euphrates River flowed nearby Eridu. The course of that river has since changed.[38]

We know the city dates back at least as far as about five thousand years ago. Unfortunately, excavations have not gone deeper for lack of funds. Still, there is evidence the city may have existed for much longer than just the excavated portion shows us.

Estimates vary, but some claim it is thousands of years older than presently believed.[39] In addition, according to Sumerian texts, Eridu was supposed to have been built by "the gods," the Anunnaki, or "Sky Guardians," as they were sometimes referred to by them.

**Sumerian Ziggurat 1**

The Amar-Sin Ziggurat positioned in the center of that most ancient of cities, the "first city," has an interesting correlation to the biblical Tower of Babel,[40] the tale of which is recorded in the Book of Genesis of the Bible. Some historians actually believe that the ziggurat was the original Tower of Babel. Let us quote just a brief passage of the text here just to refresh our memories on how this occurred:

*11 Now the whole world had one language and a*

common speech. 2 As people moved eastward, [a] they found a plain in Shinar [b] and settled there.

*3 They said to each other, "Come, let's make bricks and bake them thoroughly." They used brick instead of stone, and tar for mortar. 4 Then they said, "Come, let us build ourselves a city, with a tower that reaches to the heavens, so that we may make a name for ourselves; otherwise we will be scattered over the face of the whole earth."*

**—Genesis 11:1-9, New International Version (NIV)**

Here again, we have that very early on and very mystical association with gods/God, and reaching for the heavens on the site of an ancient structure. Such associations have endured for millennia. Eridu has had many particularly holy and supernatural connections through various mythologies and religious texts to God or the gods.

**Gilgamesh**

The city is also mentioned in the epic tale of Gilgamesh, for instance. This ancient epic is believed to be the original source story of the biblical version of the Great Flood of Noah, as well. According to Robert Ballard, the noted explorer and one of the top underwater archaeologists, the Great Flood occurred sometime around 12,000 years ago.[41] This is back to the time of Megalithia, again.

However, we are principally concerned just now with the platform. This was a large platform, and it formed the original base of the most ancient Sumerian temple, so it predates even that temple. The structure used buttresses to help support the walls of the platform, so immense was it.

Again, we have another large platform, one very ancient peoples (and we mean ancient here!) took a great deal of time, effort, and much capital expense to build in that "first city" of Eridu.

Why? Why do this when one's average life span at the time was probably in the low-thirties or less, when it took almost all of one's time just to produce enough food to feed and clothe one's self and one's family? Why would they then have spent so much of those vital resources to build something that simply doesn't seem to have been necessary, a vast huge platform?

The temple didn't require such a large foundation, so why build it that way? We've asked this same question before here, haven't we? Of course, you know what we think the answer to that question is. We think aliens caused it to be built. The site was originally an alien launch and landing platform for the Empire of Megalithia.

**Palpa Flat Mountain:** Now this one is a little different type of platform, and yet still fits the same pattern. In the Nazca region of Peru in South America, now famous for the so-called "Nazca Lines"[42] those mysterious lines that form images of a bird, spider, monkey and so much else, there is the Palpa Mountain, or Palpa Flat Mountain.[43]

The entire top portion of the mountain has literally been taken away to leave a huge, flat, surface area. Someone seems to have removed the entire top portion of the mountain to leave a vast expanse of leveled area.

What's even stranger is that no one can seem to find the debris from such an effort. One would normally assume the slopes of the mountain would be covered with talus from the removal effort of so much stone; that is, the rock and debris from such a major earth-moving effort should still be there, dumped down the slopes.

Even normal erosion would have caused this same thing, a pile of debris. What is at the top of the mountain when it erodes away should end up at the bottom, and on the sides of the slopes leading to the bottom. Gravity demands this.

Yes, water over countless years (but there is very little rainfall in this region, sometimes not for years at a time) might cut through the debris. This would leave washes and gullies coursing through the rubble, of course. Nevertheless, as anyone can plainly see with any of the mesas in Arizona, for example, there is still plenty of talus forming rough slopes of loose rock up against the side of the mountains there. Yes, drainage patterns cut through it, but the debris slopes are still very noticeable.[44]

No such debris exists at Palpa Flat Mountain, even if it was somehow due to some strange natural erosion process. It's as if someone sliced off the top and simply put it somewhere else, far away, and out of sight. Again, we have the natural erosion of the mountain's slopes there, but we do not, and cannot account for the massive amounts of rubble that should exist there after having been removed from the top of the mountain. Where did it go? Who removed it?

One thing of note; this area of Peru has a lot of naturally occurring ores. So rich is the region in this, some Peruvian mines are now in trouble for damaging the famous Nazca Lines because of their mining activities.

What are we left with here? Well, it would appear we have another huge, leveled area, a vast one, a platform of immense proportions with a mountain forming the foundation of it. This one never even had any temples built on it at all. So just what was it for? Why was it built? How was it built? Again, we think the answer must be aliens did this or had it done.

**Some Questions about these Sites**: First, let us explain that there are more such sites. However, for the purposes of this book, we merely wish to illustrate what we're talking about here with regard to huge platforms built incredibly long ago. We have neither the time nor the space to discuss all of them in this book, because it would make for a very long book, indeed. Therefore, we use these as major examples. Some questions that immediately come to mind are:

Why build such a thing in the first place? This is no minor question. The amount of effort involved in any of these undertakings, as we've illustrated earlier, is implausible by even modern-day standards. In fact, even by today's criteria, such things as moving those massive rocks of the foundation of Baalbek might still be virtually impossible to accomplish without damaging them, or could only be accomplished with a "monumental" effort on our part.

As with the Dome of the Rock and the Temple of Baalbek, the foundations predate buildings later placed upon them. In other words, the platforms weren't constructed for the later use they were put to, so their use was for something else.

Why not simply cut the stones smaller, and so be able to lift them more easily, more quickly, and certainly more conveniently? This would be the obvious way to go for any primitive people, ones whose capabilities were limited to using stone implements and later on, nascent metal instruments, such as bronze or copper with which to cut the rock. The answer would seem to be simply because they could do it, they had the capability easily to move such monstrously large chunks of stone.

Why do all these places seem to be so closely and intimately associated with myths, legends, the supernatural, religions, and often with more than just one religion? Moreover, all the sites mentioned seem to have myths and legends associated with them of the most fantastic nature, as well.

Beings supposedly ascended and descended from the heavens on such sites. Humans were taken up to the skies. Tales of wondrous devices descending or lifting with a roar of flames, smoke, and thunder, contrive to go hand-in-hand with these most ancient places.

For instance, according to Muslim beliefs, the Prophet Muhammad ascended from the Dome Of The Rock on a flying horse (one with actual wings). This occurred on what is referred to as his Night Journey to Heaven.[45] Strange rough markings in the stone, again according to Muslim tradition, are the actual imprints left behind from this feat.

As we mentioned earlier, this was the site of "the" Holy of Holies, as well. This means it was the inner sanctum of Solomon's Temple, where the Ark of the Covenant[46] was kept.

Furthermore, and again according to Muslim precepts, the Dome of the Rock is where the angel will appear to announce the Last Judgment with a trumpet blast.[47] Many of these sorts of tales surround the Dome of the Rock and the platform it was built on. All seem to have to do with heaven[48], and/or ascending or descending from it.

With regard to Baalbek, one religious legend of the region says Cain, the biblical son of the first man, Adam, built Baalbek as a fortress for his protection, and so is the oldest building in the world. Muslims in the area believe it was built by a race of demons called the djinn[49], or as we in the West know them better, genies. Others thought the platform was the result of efforts of a vanished race of giants and that King Nimrod[50] had them build it by his order.

Nimrod, if you will remember, was also the king who supposedly built the tower of Babel, in order to ascend to heaven. (Again, we have another legend or story to do with trying to go to the sky or stars. Legend also says he had been visited by Abraham, and so warned against doing this very thing. However, angry with Abraham, Nimrod had him cast into a furnace.[51] Luckily, for Abraham, he somehow managed to emerge unscathed, or at least so the story goes.

So does Baalbek have a history of the religious and supernatural surrounding it, especially with relationship to heaven or the heavens? Oh, yes, it certainly does. According to some of those legends, the events date back, clear to the beginning of humankind.

Regardless of which stories might be true or partially true, we're still left with the question: what was such a huge, gigantic, unbelievably large foundation actually used for? Why does it have so many mythical and religious connotations associated with it? Well, we think we've answered that here. Aliens had them built and aliens used them as launching sites, and as the "Landing Place."

**Chapter Conclusion**: Yes, the amount of effort involved in constructing these sites was inconceivable by even the standards of today. This is because the aliens wanted it that way, not because humans did. Yes, again, the size of the stones used was, literally, "monumental."

This idea is critical and we stress this here. It was very important to someone these platforms be built, otherwise why go through so much trouble to do it? Furthermore, since the buildings constructed on those sites in later days never required anything near like the support of such huge foundations, one can only assume the original purpose was for something else entirely, something utterly different, something alien.

The platforms were literally spaceports, landing and takeoff pads for alien rockets. Remember, Baalbek was literally referred to as "The Landing Place," and the Dome of the Rock is where God or gods spoke, and the Prophet Mohammed ascended into heaven. Add to that the Epic of Gilgamesh states that Gilgamesh actually witnessed a rocket landing on the Baalbek site, and our conclusions seem obvious.

There seems to be no other rational explanation for platforms that were built long before any other structures were placed upon them. Truly, it is hard to conceive of another reasonable use for something so grand, so monumental, and so difficult and expensive to build.

Whoever wanted platforms that *were over five million square feet in area* was willing to pay quite a high price to get them, so it wasn't meant to be an open space just to sell vegetables, fruits and meat, or to hold folk dances. No, we reiterate, these were rocket launching and landing sites.

Sound farfetched? Perhaps, but not as far-fetched as saying that people who lived 9,000 to 12,500 years ago created foundation stones so huge no modern machinery can lift them today without a terrible struggle, and only if such machines were used in very large numbers.

Given the choices, we have to ask: Which is the more likely

out of all these explanations? Did giants do the work? Did genies (djinn) or demons construct such sites? Did beings with a superior technology do it? Alternatively, did humans 9,000 to 12,500 years or more ago, somehow accomplish such a wondrous feat?

We have to go with the last idea, that humans did the actual work, but with a proviso, and that's the third idea, that they had help from a superior and alien technology. Since it would seem highly unlikely humanity of such a primitive world, or even now for that matter, could have constructed such enormous things without the aid of someone with a superior technology and capability, we feel it likely there may have been someone from "out there," who helped humankind.

Something else should be mentioned here; although there are a number of such platform sites, there are not hundreds or thousands of them. This tells us the effort was truly great, even if humans had received help from "someone" else. However, it also tells us that the supposed payoff for someone must've been great, as well. We'll discuss just what this payoff might've been in the section on technology of the Empire of Megalithia.

For now, we simply want to mention that such sites did and still do exist, and that for us, they form real evidence of "something" big going on around 9,000 to 12,500 years ago. Moreover, although the original purpose of such sites seems to be lost in antiquity, legends about their purposes still exist, and in some cases, are quite explicit, as in the Epic of Gilgamesh. In addition, the sheer size and shape of the platforms also acts as evidence in itself.

One other thing this does establish and this is important, as well. We are getting the first real signs, actual evidence of the probable age of Megalithia. The structures in question date back, far back, and in the case the Temple of Baalbek, even longer, to anywhere from 9000 to 12,500 years ago. The same holds true for the Dome of the Rock. Therefore, we now have our timeframe for Megalithia. It existed sometime during this interval, although it may have existed for some time before this.

Now we shall turn to some other evidence, evidence of a

different type of architecture of the Empire of Megalithia.

# Chapter 6

## Ancient Sites

### Other Ancient Stone Structures:

There is more we have to discuss here about stone structures besides just those monstrously large platforms, and that is the nature of some of the other types of them. Again, we must go with what is left to us from so long ago and if it wasn't made of stone, it probably no longer exists.

If this seems unlikely, well, for any of those who may have watched the various documentary shows on television about what would happen if humanity suddenly disappeared from Earth, one thing was immediately evident; all of our modern works, ones we think are so wonderful, would disappear in ten thousand years or even considerably less time. We have nothing like Baalbek, the Great Sphinx, or any such things that could withstand the test of ten thousand years, let alone a few thousand.

By the end of ten thousand years, there would be virtually nothing left to show we had ever been here, that our modern and mighty age, our global civilization, had ever existed. Our concrete buildings would not last as long as even those made of Roman concrete. You see, we don't use as good a composition. The Roman roads lasted thousands of years. Our freeways don't last decades.

Now remember, most archaeologists claim that human civilization, complete with cities, really only started anywhere from five thousand to about seven thousand, five hundred years ago. Most of them seem to like the figure of about five thousand years, give or take the better part of a thousand years.

Nevertheless, we assert Megalithia existed much longer ago than that, and that it fell sometime around 12,000 nine thousand to 9,000 B.C.E, approximately. So of course, it is incumbent upon us to try to find evidence for this having been the period of Megalithia. We have already started doing this by mentioning the huge platforms at the Temple of Baalbek and other places, and their probable dates according to mainstream archaeologists, as well as those archaeologists who differ on this viewpoint. Now we wish to discuss some other evidence for when Megalithia existed:

**Author: Klaus-Peter Simon**

**Göbekli Tepe:**[52] This is without a doubt the strangest thing we've ever come across in the way of truly ancient structures. Located in the southeastern region of Anatolia, Turkey, the site dates back at least to the Neolithic Period, some eleven thousand years ago, but perhaps even longer. Archaeologists simply aren't sure. Although, there seems to have been evidence the site was used for a very long time even prior to this dating. Some reliable archaeological sources think Göbekli Tepe was used as far back as twelve thousand years ago. This would put it well within our developing timeframe for the timespan of Megalithia.

Again, we are now well into the last Ice Age.[53] Actually, we have to qualify that statement. The last Ice Age hasn't ended, not even now, but we are talking about the time of the withdrawal of the great continental ice sheets. These once covered the northern hemisphere, and we're talking of the time when this was so. In any case, this makes the site, by some estimates, about six thousand years older than Stonehenge in England, or even more.

The inhabitants of the immediate area carved huge stones at Göbekli Tepe. They did this at a time when they had no metal implements. In other words, they were about as primitive as one can get. Their lives must've been short, harsh, and brutal in the extreme. They didn't have agriculture. Most likely, they didn't even keep animals. We are talking true nomads, primitive hunter-gatherers here.

Yet here again, we have an example of a people expending a great amount of their capital in the form of labor and effort to create such a lasting monument. This means those monuments must have been terribly important to them, because it literally meant sacrificing most of their lifespans in order to achieve the desired results.

One of the main features of Göbekli Tepe is an artificial construction known as "the Tell."[54] The Tell has a height of approximate 49 feet and is approximately 948 feet in diameter. They built this over 2,000 feet above sea level. On those columns of rock created there, were carved depictions of various animals.

Most of the animals seemed to be have been local to the region, at least at the time, but there are depictions of animals that were never native to the region. How this could be, is still unexplained. There were also depictions of stars in the carvings. Some date this star map as far back as 17,000 years ago! That's far older than even the 12,500 years we're talking about so often.

Coincidentally, this map is virtually identical to one found in one of the Lascaux Caves in France.[55] The cave paintings there, by "cavemen" date back closely to the time of Göbekli Tepe, which means that since Göbekli Tepe was an actual and major construction, then it must be just about the oldest discovered civilization so far.

While it was being built, everyone else was still huddled in dripping caves for comfort, or so historians and archaeologists would have us believe. Still, this also gives one an idea of just how primitive the people of the world were at the time. Many were still actual cave dwellers!

However, about those twin star maps found so far apart; the stars depicted would appear to be, in both maps, the Pleiades, Orion, and Taurus, among several others. There's that recurrence of Orion, as well as the Pleiades reappearing repeatedly in sites of ancient constructions. Although there are many conjectures as to why this might be, and no other equally prominent constellations used instead, nobody knows for sure. We think we may have the reason(s) and we'll discuss those later on.

Another interesting fact about Göbekli Tepe; it was deliberately buried at some point. It was hidden from view on purpose. This, too, took a good deal of effort. Nobody knows why this was done either, or exactly when. Some say it must have been to preserve or protect the site. Nobody really knows.

Nevertheless, for whatever reason, it was buried so well, that it lay hidden for thousands of years to come. Göbekli Tepe was only found in very recent times. Why was it deliberately buried, if it was? Again, we simply don't have the answers. Yes, it probably was to hide and protect it for some reason, but just what that reason may be, what threat there might have been to it, from whom, we can only surmise, and again, we have our ideas about that, too. More on that later on in the book.

**Author: Wladimir Popkov**

**Twenty-Five Thousand Year-Old "Dolmens" Found in Caucasus Region of Russia:**[56] Near the metropolis of Tzelentzchik in the Caucasus region of the Russian Federation, countless monuments have been discovered. Designated as "dolmens," nobody seems to know what these structures were used for or why they were created. However, they couldn't have been easy to construct, being made of stone as they are. They date back, variously, from 4,000 years in some cases, to as much as 25,000 years ago in other cases. These times are arrived at by several independent estimates.

Again, this puts many of them well back into the High-Empire age of Megalithia. Yes, some do argue about the age, just because these are made of stone. As we have to keep mentioning, one has a hard time telling when a stone object was constructed. Nevertheless, many archaeologists think they range over a wide span of time. Some insist that at least some of the dolmens do date back that far, to 25,000 years ago.

The structures themselves are curious things. They consist of "dressed" slabs of stone[57] and roofed over with stone, as well.

They usually have a large, very circular hole cut in the front of them, as well as an opening.

Often, they also have engravings or depictions. What the purpose of the dolmens was is still unknown. They don't seem to have been tombs, since no skeletal remains ever have been found inside of them.

That they must have been hard to construct for the people of the time is obvious. They are scattered all about the area, without any apparent plan, rhyme, or reason. There are labyrinths in the region, as well. These seem somehow to be associated with the dolmens, but again, the connection is vague. For that matter, the dolmens are of unknown origin.

Dolmens don't just exist in this area of the world. They have their "cousins," so-called underground burial chambers in places as diverse as New England, Ohio, Ireland, and England. The ones in New England are interesting because no one has any idea who created them or just how old they really are.

A final note about Dolmens; when photographs of them are taken from inside and out, often "orbs" (glowing balls of light) appear in the photos. Nobody seems to know why this is so prevalent a thing, with regard to these structures, but photographers of other megalithic sites often report the same phenomenon. That these same orbs seem to appear around crop circles and other places, as well, is an ongoing mystery, but one, which author, Hugh Newman, relates to the Earth Grid system, meaning ley lines and the power the lines generate.[58]

**Stones of Carnac:**[59] Although some say that the stones of Carnac do not all date back to the High Age of Megalithia or so we're told, they are important enough that we thought we should mention them here. General estimates are that they are around five to six thousand years old. Some argue that at least a few of them could be considerably older, and originally started at about 9,000 years ago[60].

Again, this would be during the Neolithic age. This places them in the age of the Megalithian Empire and is why we included them here. In any case, they supposedly predate the Great Pyramids of Giza by over a thousand years, according to some estimates, but not all. There are many who feel the pyramids of Giza are far older than that. Yet again, we have that constant problem of accurately estimating the age of stone structures.

Just what are the stones of Carnac? Well, we know they are made of granite. Shaped like rough-hewn monoliths, they stand, on average, slightly taller than the average human male. We know they are quite large as far as their mass goes and by all standards for such monuments, are "densely packed" together. We know there are some four thousands of them!

Incredible to conceive of such a thing, isn't it, of people

carving so many such stones? They were placed in straight lines and they seem to have some sort of representations engraved on them. As one source puts it, "subliminal faces and pictures" were carved into the upright stones.[61]

That the stones seem to have something to do with ley lines also seems apparent.[62] Again, nobody's sure as to how, but there does seem to be a definite connection based on various and numerous sources we've researched. Please follow endnote links for further information on this.

Finally, nearby stones on an island literally march down into the sea. They were placed there long enough ago that the sea level was substantially lower at the time. We know this has to have been thousands of years ago, very close to when the ice sheets retreated and so added their melt water to the oceans in enough quantity to raise the sea levels to the point where many of the stones are now submerged. Remember, the last retreat of such continent-crossing glaciers was about 10,000 years ago. Therefore, here would seem to be evidence for the stones to have been erected very near or during the time of Megalithia.

**Gunung Padang, Java**: [63] The maximum-recorded age estimate of this site based on carbon dating is 10,900 years B.C.E. This makes this site just about 13,000 years old, and places it well into in the age of Megalithia.[64] Others say it isn't as old, but even they claim estimates of from 4,700 to 1,000 B.C.E. Still others claim it goes as far back as 20,000 years! Constructed from a hillside, it's described as having been a "pyramid," built into a series of terraces with lots of megaliths at the upper end. We mean "lots" of megaliths. Please refer to the photo(s) of the site to get an idea of just how many there are.

Some claim the pyramid is the oldest and most extensive megalithic site so far ever discovered. Hundreds, perhaps even thousands of slabs of rock lie tumbled everywhere. Whoever built this spent a great deal of time, great effort, and expended a prodigious amount of energy to accomplish the task. Although it's supposed to have been constructed well before the invention of written language, one scholar said it couldn't have been done without "literacy," because of the complexity of the structure.

So who had a written language so long ago? Who was building such a tremendous edifice, carving all that rock, creating all those stones so many millennia ago? Remember, even if one were to take the time estimate most recent to us, that at the very least, still would make the pyramid twice as old as the Giza Pyramids, as their age is claimed by various Egyptologists.

However, based on so many other estimates, we believe the structure must have been constructed during the actual time of Megalithia, itself. This is because most of those estimates state this time length. We simply go with the "majority" in this case.

Puma Punku, Author: Janikorpi

Tiahuanaco, Author: Dennis Jarvis

**Tiahuanaco and Puma Punku Bolivia:**[65] In Bolivia, on the south shore of Lake Titicaca is a site known as Tiahuanaco.

Most of us are aware of this one. We mention it for a number of reasons. First, the site is old! Secondly, it is megalithic in nature. Third, it shows a level of expertise in its construction that's astonishing even by today's standards. Fourth, something catastrophic happened there. Finally, fifth, the ruins are in an area that is rife with strange legends and stranger sightings.

Arthur Posnansky, a noted Polish engineer, estimates the probable age of Tiahuanaco is about fourteen to fifteen thousand years. This is based on a number of pieces of evidence he cites to prove his case. This includes, but is not limited to, the amount of time that's passed based on the current tilt of the Earth, since the structure was originally aligned to true north and south. Since the time the ruins were new, the tilt of the Earth has deviated from this at a steady rate. This amount of deviation gives Posnansky the age of Tiahuanaco. If true, this puts the site well into the time of Megalithia.

In addition, toxodons, an extinct species of animal, are depicted in some of the ruins. These animals were supposed to have gone the way of the Dodo Bird back in the Pleistocene era, some twelve thousand years ago. This, too, would give us a fair approximation of its age, as being at least that old. This puts the structure well into the time of Megalithia.

Weirdly, native tribesmen of the area as far back as 1533 B.C.E. claimed the edifices had been built in just one night. Other legends claimed that some type of sound was used to float the stones through the air and into position.[66] These legends also bear a suspicious resemblance to ones found in Egyptian hieroglyphics that say stones there were made to float, as well, in order to build the pyramids.[67] Coincidence? If so, it's a major one.

So is this just another site with a bunch of rough-hewn stones lying about the landscape? Not hardly! The stones at this site are often referred to as "H" blocks. If you look at the picture included here, the reason for this name is largely self-evident.

However, not so evident in the picture is the extreme precision of how these blocks were cut. Many engineers will tell you they look machined and point to aspects of the stones to prove it.

There are straight grooves that are incredibly precise. These are cut into the living rock and are incredibly smooth, well-shaped ones. We have no idea what they were used for or why.

Moreover, there are perfectly drilled holes that pass right through the stones, as well. When we say these look as if they are machine precision in style, we mean it! Engineers have tried to reconstruct the rocks in order to figure out why they were built the way they were and how.

The big question is what was the purpose of them? Walls don't usually require such elaborate machining nor do they need grooves or holes in them as these "H" blocks have. Their purpose is something of a real mystery.

All this tooling, machining, and drilling of the stones would seem to have been unnecessary. That is, unnecessary for any reason we can think of. There is another quality about the stones, too. They almost look as if they might've been prefabricated. Finally, there is not only the question of why these stones were so precisely machined and drilled in appearance to be made so identical to each other, but also how this was done. We simply don't know.

The stones at Puma Punku,[68] just a short distance from Tiahuanaco, are scattered about as if some giant swung his hand and knocked them around like Lego blocks. The resulting chaos makes it look very much as if some cataclysm caused this. There are even signs of flooding, as if somehow, Lake Titicaca had sent a tsunami through this area.

One possible explanation could have been a devastating earthquake. Another popular theory is the idea of a meteor strike nearby, perhaps in the lake, itself, which caused a wave to flood the nearby land, destroying Puma Punku.

We have our own explanation. We think another cause may be behind this; a worldwide war and/or deliberate impacts by small asteroids/meteors used as kinetic weapons. We will cite evidence for this later on. However, regardless of what the cause was, something devastating did happen at the site. This seems manifestly self-evident. One just has to look at the scene to see something big happened there.

Where did the stone blocks come from? Who built this city, or whatever it was, and when? We're not sure. Some experts in the field say the native Aymara Indians built Puma Punku. However, these native people, age-old residents of the area, say they had nothing to do with it. They claim creatures with the ability to "fly" strange machines built the place.

Oddly, as if to back their statement, these native people seem to have no history of having built such structures in any way, shape, or form, or over any amount of time, whatsoever. If they ever had this knowledge, it is long gone, utterly vanished from their culture and racial memory. Once again, they claim they never had such knowledge in the first place. So who did?

One other interesting fact about the stones at Tiahuanaco; they are fitted together so well, that not even a razor blade or piece of paper can be slipped between the joints. What's more, the rocks have an almost rounded look to them. Some claim they might have been melted into place, or that somehow the surface tension of the stone was broken to allow them to be more fluid and so flow together to fit more precisely. We don't know if this is so, but just how they achieved such an incredibly tight fit for the stones remains an enigma to this day.

As always, the age of the structures is difficult to ascertain. Archaeologists, based largely on what they feel is the history of the area, try to place the edifices' creation in much more recent times. They do this relying on the timeline they've developed for this region. In other words, the archaeologists are only guessing, and that guess is based on very little actual evidence, indeed. However, despite their claim local indigenous people built them, those people themselves thoroughly refute this idea.

Actually, the stones seem to date from various historical periods, based on different researchers' results. The estimates by some of them begin at about 9,000 to 10,000 years ago. Some claim even older dates, as far back as twenty-five thousand years ago, or even more. The fact that we can find such similar stones and structures around the world, yet again demonstrates the global nature of Megalithia. What's more, it gives us further evidence for a timeframe of the Empire. We're beginning to narrow this down now.

**Sunken Yonaguni Monument:**[69] This massive and pyramidal-shaped, terraced structure off the coast of Japan, just south of the Ryukyu Islands, although controversial in aspects, is considered by many to have been artificially constructed or at least artificially altered as many scientists believe. Not all of the natural structure needed such altering. The nature of the rock is such that it only had to be worked somewhat to achieve the results the builders desired.

So although perhaps a natural formation in essence, work seems to have been definitely done to it. Many date that work back to about 10,000 years ago. Perfectly straight grooves cut into the stone, and what appear to be deliberately constructed archways, show that human hands, or somebody's "hands," altered the rock in terraces in various ways.

The fact that the type of workmanship at the monument resembles closely that of some very ancient works on dry land in the same region does seem to suggest this structure isn't entirely natural by any means. When was this done? Well, based on how much the sea levels have risen in this area, to a level where the base of the pyramid is just over 100 feet below the surface of the ocean, that would make it at least 10,000 years ago, or perhaps even longer when the structure was still completely on dry land. This easily puts it into the age of the Megalithian Empire.

**Author: Wknight94**

**The Great Sphinx:**[70] Ah, the eternal riddle of the great Sphinx! How this has plagued humanity down through the centuries. Most mainstream archaeologists believe the Sphinx to have been built at sometime around 2,500 B.C.E. Nevertheless, this is one of the hottest controversies in archaeology today.

Others claim the Sphinx is far older. One scientist in particular, Robert M. Schoch,[71] a geologist, has done much to sub-stantiate his claim the Sphinx dates back at least 7,000 to 9,000 years, or perhaps, even more. He bases this on the erosion patterns water has created around and on the Sphinx. He also bases it on another anomaly with respect to the Sphinx, itself, and this is the fact the face appears to have been reworked, because the head is now too small for the proportions of the body. In other words, later people altered the original look of the Sphinx.

With regard to the water erosion patterns, which he says are quite distinct from wind or sand erosion patterns, and which we personally know to be a fact, since we've studied geology, as well, they prove (according to him) the Sphinx to be the much greater age he claims.

For one thing, there is very little rain in the area of the great Sphinx today and there hasn't been for millennia. So the normal amount of rainfall on an annual basis that they do have, would have been insufficient over the last millennia to have caused this much erosion by water in so relatively short a time. Although the dry wind has eroded many things, it cannot account for the particular type of erosion patterns done to the Sphinx by what can only have been water destruction.

Therefore, based on his assessments, he believes the Sphinx to be far more ancient than most archaeologists say. He further argues the structure has to date back to a time when there was more average rainfall.

Where does that place the time of the Sphinx's creation? Well, we do know that during and shortly after the last Ice Age, there was more rainfall in the region. So for this much water damage to have accumulated, the Sphinx must date back to that time of just about 10,000 years ago. If Robert Schoch is correct, this places the Sphinx back in the time of Megalithia, and long before civilization was supposed to have started or been capable of such feats.

**Author: MichelV**

**Great Pyramids of Giza:**[72] The Pyramids of Giza are very unusual phenomena. If ever there were any arguments or mysteries swirling about something, they are the epitome of such conversation pieces. Controversy about them has been intense and ongoing for decades. Controversy still rages and promises to continue to do so for the near future.

Originally thought to have been built around 2,500 B.C.E. (about 4,500 years ago), and with many archaeologists still adhering to this idea, there seem to be many questions and arguments about that assumption. As always, stone is hard to date to a precise time. As usual in such cases, archaeologists go by what they dig up around them, and what they think they know of the timeline of the history of the region.

This can be misleading. For instance, if at some point the Pyramids were covered with sand, and we know this has happened in the past, but then subsequently cleared away again, it would appear they had been built at the time those implements would've been found that helped in the clearing. The implements wouldn't just be shovels or brooms. They'd be all sorts of things for cleaning up those mighty structures. Unless the archaeologists dug deeper, they'd never know any difference. This is a problem in and of itself. At the very least, it can confuse dating of the time of their construction.

Many also strongly question the purpose of the Pyramids, why they were built. The claim by Egyptologists that they are tombs of pharaohs has some seriously major flaws inherent in them. First, there is no sign the pyramids ever were used for this purpose originally, as being created as tombs for pharaohs.

There aren't any of the usual elaborate hieroglyphics on the walls to act as prayers and magical incantations to aid the pharaoh in passing to the next life. Nor are there the usual illustrations showing some dead Pharaoh being translated to the afterlife. There is nothing at all along these lines.[73]

The chambers archaeologists suggestively named for other burial tombs, are not the same size, shape, or seem to have been put to the same purposes as those other structures we know to be tombs. Neither do these chambers contain any hieroglyphic, as all the other tombs do. Never has any sign of funerary equipment been found there either, not a stick, stone, or Canopus jar lid.

There are a few hieroglyphics,[74] but these are hidden in a tiny shaft and only recently have been uncovered. They are highly controversial, because nobody knows quite how they could have been placed there. Some claim they are a hoax. Written in red paint, they amount to but a few words and really explain nothing at all.

So were the pyramids tombs? We, along with many others, think not. There truly seems to be little actual evidence for such a conclusion. What we do think happened is that Egyptologists do what many archeologists do. That is, they sometimes try to force such things to fit the existing "facts," as they see them, the timeline they believe to be the correct one. To do this, they sometimes truly leap to some rather unsubstantiated conclusions, as with the pyramids being tombs for pharaohs, when there seems to be no evidence to back this viewpoint.

Recently, the questions about this subject have grown with

the discovery of new spaces, chambers, and shafts in the pyramids. Some of these are very strange, indeed, and their purposes appear almost unfathomable, especially if one regards the pyramids as being just tombs.

For example, there has been the discovery of the "Gantenbrink's Door."[75] This was found in the Southern Shaft.[76] They discovered another door at the Northern Shaft, in the Queen's Chamber.[77] These are very atypical features and are found nowhere else in any other tombs or ancient buildings of Egypt. Their purpose also is a major puzzle, because it isn't believed they were "doors" in the actual sense of the term at all.

There are other peculiar features. For instance, in a book by Chris Dunn, *The Giza Power Plant,* Mr. Dunn, who is an engineer, states there is considerable evidence for the idea of an explosion having occurred in the pyramid sometime in the distant past. It would seem some of the stones in one area of the pyramid do not match the quality, size, or shape of the rest of the pyramid, and so would seem to have been replacement stones, "woven in" after the fact. According to him, this was in order to repair the damage from an explosion.

In addition, there are noticeable fissures in the granite supports of the southeastern portion of the ceiling of a room. Some say this was due to earthquake damage. Yet, there is no corresponding damage in any other portions of the pyramid adjacent to this area to corroborate this idea. If an earthquake, the damage was unbelievably restricted to just one area and this in a pyramid whose stonework and structure were the same throughout. This would tend to lend further credence to the idea of an explosion occurring in just one portion of the pyramid.

In addition, in the so-called King's Chamber,[78] the walls and floor of that area seem to be separating, appear to have been forced outward, as if from an explosive blast from within. The erroneously called "sarcophagus" in the room, is discolored, being a dark brown, rather than the original, rose-colored granite typical of the quarry from which it was hewn, and typical of such items found elsewhere.

This discoloration could very well be from intense heat, causing a chemical reaction, and thus a change in the surface color of the stone. Furthermore, the "so-called "sarcophagus" is like no other. It certainly is not like those of any other pharaohs, and many believe it isn't meant to be such a thing at all.

By the way, this is the only "evidence" Egyptologists use to try to prove the pyramid was a tomb. Not much, is it, to back such a claim? What happened to needing more corroboration for such a premise?

As usual with this book, there is more. There are narrow shafts, much too small for any human to enter. Recently a documentary was done exploring these with a specially made tiny robot to climb inside of them. These strange shafts had some sort of doors, or seals part way up inside of them. How this was even accomplished is yet another enigma. These "doors" were composed of small limestone blocks and had copper fittings embedded into them. Why?

How this was done is simply unknown. The purpose for these is completely unknown, as well. Some want to call them airshafts, but with interior partitions stopping the air from flowing, what good would they have served for supplying air? Besides this, the shafts didn't run all the way to the outside. So how would air get in? There would have to have been some sort of pumping mechanism for any real quantity of air to be forced through such tiny shafts, and nothing of this sort, or anything like it has ever been discovered. Most peculiarly, no other pyramids have these "airshafts."

No, given all this information, they simply can't have been constructed as airshafts, because if they were, they were flat out too small and too blocked by those "doors" to have accomplished anything at all in the way of airflow. Truly, the idea is ludicrous.

There is one more thing. Although much has been said about the pyramids, and we simply don't have the room here to discuss it all, it is important to note that one of the shafts, a southern one in the King's Chamber aims up at the constellation of Orion. Here's the clincher: the shaft does not aim at the constellation's present position, but where it would have appeared in the night skies at least 12,000 years ago! Once more, we have that 12,000-year number.

Yes, there is even more! If one takes an aerial view of the Pyramids of Giza, along with the Nile River, it mirrors the constellation of Orion, including all the main stars of the "belt" that we see from Earth, and with the Nile River forming the Milky Way.[79] We don't mean there is a vague resemblance; we mean it seems to coincide with the actual constellation point for point with the bigger pyramids representing the bright, major stars, and smaller structures representing the visually smaller stars.

Here's a breakdown of the similarities:

**1.** The three main stars of Orion's Belt are slightly out of position, and so not in an actual straight line in the sky. One star, the smallest of the three is positioned slightly more to the East than the others. The pyramids exactly reflect this misalignment in their layout.

**2.** The three pyramids all skew toward the southwest. This matches the visual pattern of Orion's Belt in the sky.[80]

**3.** The placement of the pyramids, the positioning of them in relation to the Nile River is a mirror image of the actual Constellation of Orion's positioning in the night sky with regard to the Milky Way.

**4.** The pyramids and the Great Sphinx were at their best alignment with the Constellation of Orion on the Giza Plateau in the year 10,450 B.C.E. In other words, the Sphinx and the three Pyramids of Giza would have exactly aligned on the ground with Orion's Belt 12,450 years ago, approximately.

What does this mean? Well, it certainly implies the pyramids were not the product of individual pharaohs building them where and when they wished, or to whatever size suited their own particular needs. The complex interrelationship of the pyramids and the Great Sphinx, the way they emulate the Constellation of Orion in so many ways, and did this at their best over 12,000 years ago can be no accident.

Therefore, the pyramids were built with this in mind for the very beginning. They were designed and executed according to some comprehensive master plan that may have spanned lifetimes (or not, if aliens helped to build them) and to which successive pharaohs had to go along with. This would seem to be in direct contradiction to Egyptologists' explanations for them and shows they were built millennia before the the timeline given to us by today's Egyptologists.

Of course, this puts the construction of the Sphinx, as well as the Pyramids of Giza, in the time of the Megalithian Empire.

**Chapter Conclusion:** Ample evidence exists that cities of stone, various stone structures, megaliths, if you will, existed in places around the world and date back anywhere from 8,000 to 25,000 or more years ago. Again, the dates necessarily vary. This is because of the nature of our dating systems. Even so, this puts them all in, or very close to the time of the Empire of Megalithia.

Since these structures are real, we have logically to assume there was some type of civilization capable of producing them at those times, at times, which were said to be millennia before civilization was supposed to have begun. That mystery civilization had capabilities we don't fully understand. We choose to call that civilization, Megalithia.

There is something else to consider, as well. Whoever built these things loved using stone. Yes, it was a readily available material at a time when different building materials and sources for them were rare. However, it was by no means the easiest material to work with at the time. Wood, for instance, would have been far easier. The ancient forests of Earth had barely been touched yet, so there was plenty of timber to be had, and it would have been far easier to work with than stone.

Here is the crux of the matter. The more primitive the civilization, the harsher the realities are for its citizens. We repeat this here for emphasis. There is little produced in such cultures in the way of capital excess. Almost all goes to support a life that is mostly a matter of basic subsistence, of scrabbling every single day to find enough food, shelter, and clothing just in order to survive that day.

Given the brutal conditions of existence, then, it strikes us as very strange so many people scattered about the planet would spend so much time and effort, and we are talking a great deal of effort here, in building these stone structures. Why do we stress this point? Well, because it is just so astonishing. It defies reason or logic that they would normally resort to doing this—creating buildings that we now claim were largely ceremonial and/or religious in nature, or just as tombs, and so added nothing to the physical improvement of those peoples' lives, or their daily survivability. It just doesn't make good sense.

If you were going to build anything that strong, wouldn't you build a fort, or citadel, to protect yourselves, and not just vast open platforms, for instance? Even temples to their gods would be understandable, but platforms?

These stone structures, these megaliths, were not places for people to live. Apparently, the citizenry of Megalithia were relegated to mud and daub wattle huts, stick buildings, or mud-brick homes. These sorts of primitive edifices did not last, of course. They have vanished over the thousands of years that have passed since then. Mud and straw brick crumbled to dust. Wood rotted away. No, not for them, the common people were the millennia-lasting, megalithic, stone edifices used as dwelling places.

One wouldn't do this, that is expend such time and energy on something of so little use, unless someone was forcing them to do it, or they had a great belief that this was worthwhile, that someone had coerced them into believing this was so. "Somebody" in control of these various peoples around the world was ordering them to build these things at great personal sacrifice to the laborers involved. The overlords probably told them this was the will of the gods (aliens?). They offered some limited help and aid in the form of their technological capacity. We have distorted legends handed down by different cultures that this may have happened.

For instance, with the Temple of Solomon, King Solomon could supposedly command "demons." By controlling them, he had his temple built far faster than he could have otherwise done. Tales tell of humans working on it by day, and those "demons" of his by night. He was also supposed to have had a "flying carpet," which he used to get to other places in a hurry.

Of course, we don't think it was a true flying carpet, any more than an alien UFO is really a "flying saucer." Whatever it was that King Solomon might have used, the closest thing the populace could compare it to, was that of a "flying carpet."

With Baalbek, either giants or genies were supposed to have helped create the platform. As to which, depends on which sources of legends one chooses. Again, we have multiple legends some sort of supernatural or supernormal help to construct these colossal monuments.

In addition and as mentioned earlier, in ancient Egyptian lore, the same sort of thing occurs. Hieroglyphics state that the workers had the help of something that made the huge blocks of limestone float, as if by magic. In fact, they called it magic.

Even so, we authors think humans, just like us, accomplished much of the brute work. Consider it slave labor, if you will. In our opinion, that's what it amounted to being, if not actually just that. We believe these edifices were built at the behest of the aliens and had their technological support to aid them in these endeavors.

So not only do megalithic structures tell us what type of buildings were popular during the age of Megalithia and what the approximate time span of the Empire might have been, based on dating those structures, but it also tells us something else. That is, the state and condition of the peoples who existed in that Empire. One more thing, it also gives us an approximation of when Megalithia ended. This was when the worldwide building of megaliths so suddenly and abruptly ceased.

In addition, it would appear the world had rulers, since someone had to coordinate these edifices all over the world, see them constructed. Those rulers demanded constructions be built and damn the human cost in doing it, apparently. The local populations would seem to have had little choice in the matter. They had to do as their overlords bid them. Because if they had a choice, they probably wouldn't have spent so much time and energy, creating something that served no real earthly purpose for them, personally. We wouldn't have these great constructions dotting the landscape today.

Yes, some structures might have been religious in design or have been used as calendars to help people to know the planting seasons, but a great many of the stone structures seem not to have served that kind of purpose at all. They had no such apparent function. The great stone platforms are an example of this. Göbekli Tepe is another, as is the Great Sphinx, and the Great Pyramids of Giza, among many others.

We still really don't know what the pyramids were truly for, or why they went to such length, over such a great deal of time to construct them to resemble the Orion Constellation, complete with the Nile River mirroring the Milky Way.

The pyramids certainly didn't help the people of the time to till their fields. They didn't aid them to grow crops, or maintain herds of animals. They didn't even tell them when to do this.

In fact, they detracted from the population's available time to grow their crops. Simple logic: If you were facing starvation at that time, which would you have chosen to do, to grow crops or build massive stone structures? Especially, when the latter choice meant you would probably starve and die an early death as a result? The answer seems obvious—you'd choose not to bother to build such edifices. Since the people built these things, despite this, then we believe it was because they had little or no choice in the matter.

Another point is many of the structures seem even to pre-date the invention of agriculture. Therefore, the people who built them must have been hunter-gatherers, very primitive peoples, indeed. How would such have the knowledge, the skills, the abilities, and the learned artisanship even to build such structures without help? What would they have used for tools? It seems an unlikely scenario. Ergo, they must have had help.

Finally, we now get the first hints they did have help, and that help was of such a wondrous nature that the people of the time, no matter their location on Earth, or which structure we talk about, considered that help to be nothing short of miraculous, or "magic." This gives us a good indication Megalithia may have had technologies and capabilities, at least on the part of its rulers, to do things humans simply couldn't comprehend, short of subscribing them to "demons," "genies," or "giants." Therefore, Megalithia seems to have had access to a truly advanced type of technology, perhaps even well beyond our own. We will delve into this topic further, later on.

# Chapter 7

## Drowned Cities and Lost Civilizations of Megalithia

**D**rowned cities and lost civilizations;[81] we've all heard stories of different ones. Perhaps the most famous is Atlantis. Others you may have heard of include Lemuria (sometimes called and/or confused with Mu), Mu (believed by some to be the mother civilization of Lemuria), as well as the drowned city of Ys. There are many more such tales. The number of supposedly drowned cities almost borders on being phenomenal. Of course, there is more evidence to support the idea of some of these places having actually existed, than with regard to others. Let's look at some of the main ones:

**The city of "Ys," also known as "Is:"**[82] This one may not ring a bell with you, but it was considered so beautiful, that another city, said to be similar in beauty and sophistication to it, was named for it. "Par Ys" or "Par Is" in an old Breton dialect means, literally, "like Ys" or "like Is." We know the city that was like it, as the city of "Paris," France.[83] Interesting, isn't it?"

The city was said to have been located inside a large dike that held back the sea and so protected the metropolis from the waters of the Douarnenez Bay, according to legend. What lends some extra credence to this supposedly mythical city is there are roads in Breton, France, ancient ones, which later the Romans had even used for themselves. Some of these lead down to the seashore and go straight on into the water. Did these roads once lead to a now sunken city? Was it Ys?

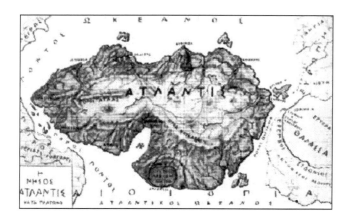

**Atlantis:**[84] First, do we know if Atlantis really existed? Yes, we think we do. Either Atlantis itself, or something approximating it, probably did exist in some fashion. Plato specifically mentions the city in one of his works, written in about 370 B.C.E.

He describes Atlantis as having been a beautiful place, and highly advanced technologically. He speaks of the city as having been on a very large island with circular canals in the city proper. However, he never explains the location of Atlantis.

The result is there are many places where different people think Atlantis may have been located. The controversies have raged and will continue to rage over that particular aspect of the subject for some long time to come, no doubt.

Finding the location of Atlantis is made even harder by the fact that Plato said the city was destroyed in one night, and sank beneath the sea. People have looked everywhere around the globe trying to locate the site.

Some say it was the island of Santorini[85] in the Mediterranean. Others say Atlantis lie off the island of Bimini, and point to what seems to be an artificial structure there known as the Bimini

Road. Even spiritualists and clairvoyants have had a hand in trying to locate Atlantis. Edgar Casey said it would be found beneath the sea somewhere near Bermuda. Oddly, the Bimini Road would qualify as such a location.

Other possible sites for Atlantis include just about anywhere one can imagine, including Mexico, off the coast of England, and even in South America. Some even say that deep beneath the sea, off the coast of Cuba, are what look like ruins of the lost city.

The interesting thing to note about Atlantis is how quickly its demise came upon it. This is a theme we see constantly repeated with lost lands and lost cities, that they were destroyed sometimes, literally, overnight." The idea that something of that size could be destroyed in just twenty-four hours or less would normally seem to be impossible, unless it was a cataclysmic earthquake, or a volcano on the order of a caldera like the one at Santorini.

Another interesting thing about Atlantis is when the cataclysm was supposed to have taken place. Plato says the island existed up until about 10,000 B.C.E. This places Atlantis right during the period of Megalithia, putting it at about 12,000 years ago.

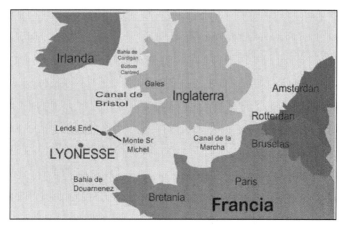

**Author: Robin222**

**Lyonesse:**[86] With its origins in Celtic legend, Lyonesse was supposed to be a kingdom near Cornwall in the southwest of England. It is also known as being the home of Tristan, of the famous Tristan and Iseult fame, as in the Wagnerian opera, *Tristan and Isolde*.[87] This city was said to have sunk beneath the waves.

As with the City of Ys, it is said that during storms, one can hear the bells of the city ringing beneath the waves. Lyonesse could well be (in our opinion), a separate tale from that of Ys, but still speaking of the same original sunken city. Is the city real or just a legend? Well, if just a legend, it is a very persistent and detailed one.

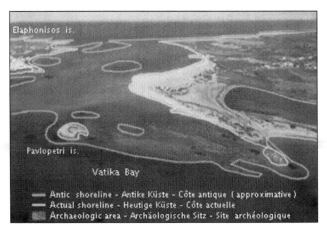

Author: Spiridon Ion Cepleanu

**Pavlopetri:**[88] This 5,000-year-old, full-sized city originally settled by Greeks, is probably the most ancient city beneath the waves, and its existence is a fact. Before it sank beneath the sea, Pavlopetri was a true city of the times. Homes, temples, tombs, courtyards, and even roads have been discovered, and all have resided underwater for 5,000 years now. What sent that city to the bottom of the sea so long ago?

**Author: Hanay**

**Atlit-Yam, Israel:**[89] Over a half mile out into the Mediterranean and not far from Haifa, Israel, a very ancient town lies beneath the sea. The town or large village covers an area of about 430,557 square feet and dates back to 7,000 B.C.E. This means the village was at least 9,000 years old, and so places it in the time of Megalithia.

Atlit-Yam constitutes one of the largest and oldest submerged settlements. Nevertheless, because the streets are not laid out in any organized pattern, it is referred to as a village rather than a city. Even so, many of the inhabitants lived in good-sized stone homes with courtyards and even paved floors.

**Last Temple Still On Shore, Author: Leah**

**Mahabalipuram:**[90] The sunken old city of Mahabalipuram and the extensive ruins there have created something of a "thing" in the archeological world. Why? Because such tales of a sunken city had always been considered mere legends, myths, and nothing more. The discovery of Mahabalipuram (not to be confused with the more modern city on land), in Tamil Nadu, India, has once more brought up the idea of the Great Flood. Local oral legends told of seven splendid temples. One day, six of them drowned beneath the sea. The seventh temple still survives on shore.

The intriguing part of sunken Mahabalipuram is the legends say this wondrous city was a victim of the gods, who destroyed it out of envy. They caused a great flood to sink it beneath the sea. The city supposedly sank beneath the waves sometime around 1,200 to 1,500 years ago, but the city itself was far older than that.

One more thing; this sunken city begs a question. That is, if one such city beneath the waves was always thought to be nothing more than the product of legends and pure myths, but was then found to actually exist, might not the same hold true for some of the other more legendary sunken cities, as with Atlantis, for instance?

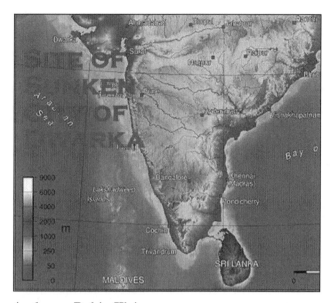

**Author:    Robin Klein**

**Bay of Cambay (Presently referred to as the Gulf of Khambhat:**[91] An extensive underwater site of a massive 9,500-year-old city has been discovered in the Gulf of Khambhat. Seemingly, endless square miles of structures, numerous ruins exist at the site, along with pottery shards and even human remains. The age of this city places it well within the time of Megalithia, and so this submerged city predates any other discoveries in the region by well over 5,000 years.

Why is this significant? Because it places tremendous pressure on historians to reconsider when human civilization began in this area of the world, something they and archaeologists are loathe wanting to do. The city has been named "Dwarka," which means 'Golden City,' and was named for a metropolis that is said to have existed in the sea and which belonged to the god, Krishna, a prominent god of the Hindu religion.

One last thing with regard to "Dwarka;" it could be the origin of the legend of the lost land of Lemuria, which many say existed in either the Pacific or Indian Oceans.

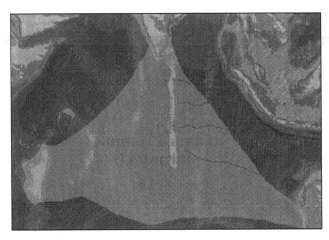

**Author: Dbachmann**

**Lemuria:**[92] There is some confusion with regard to this legendary lost land. Some say another name for it is "Mu," while others insist Mu was a separate lost land. Lemuria is said to be a continent or large body of land that sank beneath the ocean and so the civilization was lost.

If this seems farfetched, please consider there really are sunken continents. Zealandia is a submerged continent in the Pacific, along with Mauritia. In the Indian Ocean is the Kerguelen Plateau. Any of these, or even just the highest portion on one of them, might have been home to Mu or Lemuria. So perhaps the idea of Atlantis, for instance, isn't quite as unbelievable as one may at first think.

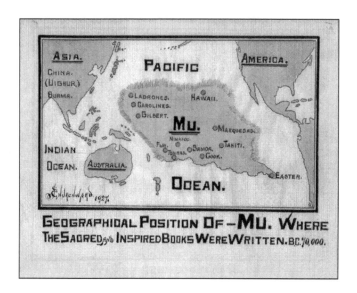

GEOGRAPHICAL POSITION OF – MU. WHERE THE SACRED & INSPIRED BOOKS WERE WRITTEN. B.C. 70,000.

**Mu:**[93] Mu, like Lemuria (and they may well have been the same), was supposedly a lost continent, and which then sunk beneath the waves at the dawn of human civilization. If this happened, it would place Mu and its destruction, as with Lemuria, right around the time of Megalithia. Augustus Le Plongeon, a writer in the 19th century, believed that Egypt and the civilizations in Mesoamerica were created, or founded by survivors of the Mu catastrophe.

Is their actual evidence for Mu, like Lemuria, that other lost continent, existed? Very little, but as shown above, there are such things, as lost continents. Sunken cities thought to be legendary have turned out to be quite real, so we feel the jury may still be out on these two lost lands.

**Chapter Conclusion:** As is obvious in this chapter, we have included both so-called mythical cities and lands, along with ones that were found to be quite real, actual sunken cities. Our purpose here is to show that legends and myths sometimes really are fact, that it is often hard to determine which is which, until the actual sites of such places are discovered.

We've also shown that actual submerged continents do exist and this is according to mainstream geology. Furthermore, we've demonstrated that some of the sunken cities discovered date back to the time of Megalithia.

Therefore, if enough legends persist about certain places and lost civilizations, perhaps one can conclude there might be some truth to at least some of those legends. In any case, since numerous real sunken cities have been found, and since some do date back to the time of Megalithia, and since all are coastal cities, one must conclude that something happened around 9,000 to 12,000 years ago, give or take 1,000 years. That something, whatever it was, affected coastal regions around the world.

Almost every culture in the world has some version of the legend of the Great Flood. We feel this is no coincidence. Combined with the sunken cities, both real and legendary, the legend of the Great Flood makes for a powerful argument that something like it actually occurred. So one can't help but think that something momentous did.

What can we derive from this information?

1. Actual cities were inundated around the time of the end of Megalithia. There is solid archaeological evidence for this fact.

2. Many of the cities were said to have been destroyed by the gods, either out of jealousy, or because the cities were corrupted in the viewpoint of those gods. The biblical account of Sodom and Gomorrah is another good example of this.

3. To this day, civilizations around the world have the myth and/or the religious belief that a Great Flood occurred long ago. Now in these last years, there seems to be some actual evidence to support this idea.

4. Whatever happened appears to have happened very quickly. This is no slow gentle drowning of coastal regions due to the ice caps melting on a gradual basis. The legends of the Great Flood, the myths of all those submerged cities, the real ones, all say that whatever

happened transpired quickly, often in a day or less. Why should we believe such myths? Well, the legends of Mahabalipuram, of that submerged city, turned out to be real. So why should the legend of how quickly the destruction of that city occurred be any less real?

Now, having established that Megalithia most likely existed, let's move on to what the Empire might've actually been like. The following chapters will give some in-depth ideas of what life was actually like in Megalithia.

# Chapter 8

## Could Megalithia Have Lasted
## an Incredible Amount of Time?

L ike most things, Megalithia may have evolved. That is to say, in the beginning, it wasn't what it was at the end. In addition, we have had some interesting, tantalizing hints that aliens may have been on earth for a very long time. For instance, one estimate of the Dashka Stone, otherwise known as the Map of the Creator[94] date it as being possibly as much as 120 million years old. However, there are other hints that aliens may have been on earth a very long time ago. Here are just some examples.

**Radioactive T-Rex**
**Author: InSapphoWeTrust**

**Aliens and Dinosaurs:**[95] Dinosaurs and aliens wouldn't seem to have anything in common, would they? Yet, ancient alien theorists think otherwise. They point to the fact that the bones of many types of dinosaurs, among them Tyrannosaurus Rex, are highly radioactive.[96] So radioactive are some of the skeletons that museums have had to paint them with a lead-based paint in order to protect people from any harmful effects of the radiation. So, were dinosaurs wiped out by a nuclear war, rather than an asteroid?

Sounds like a strange question, doesn't it? However, perhaps it isn't. Laid down at the time of the destruction of the dinosaurs, some 65 million years ago, geologists have found a thin layer of iridium[97] in the Earth's rock. They point out that despite being exceedingly rare as far as naturally occurring on Earth, iridium is found in asteroids, and so this layer is a possible sign that an asteroid destroyed the dinosaurs.

However, there is one other known source of iridium, and that happens to be thermonuclear weapons. So, could a nuclear war have killed off the dinosaurs? It would account for so many of the skeletons being so highly radioactive. Moreover, if this did happen, then it took place approximately 65,000,000 years ago. Were aliens on Earth then, for whatever reasons? It could well have been so. Aliens may come and go all the time and they may already have done this many times throughout the history of our planet.

Are we saying that it is actually certain that 65 million years ago there was a thermonuclear war? No, we aren't. The explanation does have one added and distinct advantage over the asteroid one. That is, it not only accounts for the death of the dinosaurs just as effectively as the asteroid would have, but it also accounts for why the skeletons of so many of them are highly radioactive. In other words, it answers two questions, rather than just one. In addition, it uses the same information, that layer of iridium, to do it.

We must note here that detractors say the reason some of the skeletons are so radioactive is that they were discovered in Wyoming and Colorado, where there is naturally occurring radioactive deposits. Skeletons buried in these layers of stone logically would acquire the radiation.

Good point. We seem to have an answer, a reasonable and mundane one, as to the question of why some dinosaur skeletons are radioactive. However, quite a number of radioactive skeletons have been found that didn't come from Wyoming or Colorado or from rocks with a higher radioactive mineral content to them. So it turns out this is not a solution to the problem at all, since it doesn't begin to account for all the radioactive skeletons. Yet, a nuclear war fits all the criteria very nicely.

**Dinosaurs and People Coexisting:**[98] Further, to confuse matters, there are some other oddities. Various depictions and images of dinosaurs seem to exist in our own history. For instance, at the temple of Angor Wat, there is a bass relief with what appears to be an image of a Stegosaurus, complete with the plates running down its spine.[99] Other images from around the world show human beings intermixed with what clearly look to be dinosaurs or very large lizard-like creatures.[100]

Compounding the weirdness of all this, there are fossilized prints of what really look like human footprints right next to those of dinosaur tracks, and embedded in the same layer of rock. Some of these are in Texas. Others were found in Southwest China's Chongqing region.

Again, we aren't saying dinosaurs and people did coexist at the same time. However, something odd in the history of our planet seems to have been going on. We simply can't account for it. We'd like to be able to explain all these things away, but we can't. Still, if humans knew about dinosaurs, perhaps some few species had somehow survived the catastrophe.

Alternatively, maybe they were shown images of these creatures by the aliens. Bob Lazar,[101] the physicist that worked at Area Fifty-One, claims the government has photographs given to them by aliens of things out of history. He claims there are even photos dating from that time, the one of dinosaurs. This could be one possible explanation.

**Archaeological Anomalies:**[102] We won't go into depth on the subject here, because we already have in other books. Suffice it to say, that strange objects have been dug up in layers of coal, as well as elsewhere, that simply don't seem to belong to the time that such layers of minerals were supposedly formed. Hammers, ladles, vases, bells—all sorts of things have been found inside of lumps of coal, and other minerals.

How did they get there? There are only three possible solutions to this question. The first is they were placed there somehow and are hoaxes. If this is so, there are an incredible number of such hoaxes, and just how something like that could be accomplished, when some of the items were found over two centuries ago, is a complete mystery.

The second possible solution is time travel. Perhaps in our future, we invent time travel, travel to the past, and accidentally leave such objects behind. The final answer would be that aliens visited long ago, and they left these objects behind. There is a fourth solution. It is possible that someone or something native to the earth was intelligent enough to create and use such objects all those millions of years ago.

However, the most reasonable explanation, in our opinion, is that someone visited our planet long ago, periodically, and some of these objects were accidentally left behind. Is this the correct answer? Again, we simply don't know. Time travel, as unbelievable as that may sound, could be a viable alternative, since Einstein's theories allow for it. However, neither do we believe these are hoaxes, so somehow these anomalies have to be accounted for. We've chosen our solution. We leave you to choose yours.

**Chapter Conclusion:** Although we cannot account for all these things, why they should exist, or what they mean exactly, as we said earlier, they do offer tantalizing clues. At the very least, it hints strongly that something may have been happening on earth a very, very long time ago. This means we might have been visited often by aliens throughout the history of our planet, and on a regular basis. Megalithia may have very deep roots, indeed, in the history of our world.

From the available evidence we have that isn't quite so tantalizing, is more concrete, we think Megalithia probably reached its zenith and then collapsed sometime around 12,000 years ago. Exactly how long Megalithia may have lasted overall prior to that collapse is a matter of some conjecture. Our guess is that it could have been for thousands upon thousands of years.

# Chapter 9

## The Industry and Economy of Megalithia

In the preceding three chapters, we've demonstrated that civilization went back for much farther in time than most archaeologists were once willing to state. We've provided examples of this fact. We've even managed to supply dates from reputable sources to back this contention of ours.

Not only that, but we've pointed out that the most ancient of civilizations, Megalithia, loved the use of stone. They built to endure. They built to last. They built on a monumental level, literally.

Just why was it so important to build on such a level, though, and to create edifices that would last for millennia, is a curious thing. It would suggest that whoever the rulers were, they assumed their kind would be in power for a long, long time. They would need to use such structures for lengthy durations.

What would be the purpose of such a strange civilization, one with such dichotomies in it, and seemingly on every level of the Empire? Was it just a first and rather strange way of humans trying to survive together?

We don't think so. The social structure of Megalithia was just too "top down" in nature, and the demand for building such things seemingly too important.

Why do we insist on this point? Well, if one looks at other primitive tribal civilizations today, one doesn't see such grandiose projects being undertaken anywhere. We are referring here to those cultures that have been little influenced by the technological world. Yes, they are hard to find these days, but we know there were many such in the Twentieth Century, and there are a few left even to this day. The peoples of the upper Amazon do not build such monuments. The present-day Mountain People of New Guinea do not. Even Native Australians, so-called "Aborigines," did not indulge in such monument building.

So whether South America, islands in the Pacific and elsewhere, or Australia, or anywhere else in the world, truly primitive people, on the same level as we all were technologically speaking 10,000 years ago, show a complete lack of such constructions.

There are exceptions in history, as with the Mayans and Aztecs. Again, we think they were influenced at one time by the aliens, because their more northerly neighbors did not build such structures. Technologically speaking, these other people peaked on the East Coast of the United States with the bow and arrow, spear, and tomahawk, along with birch-bark canoes. However, areas influenced by the aliens saw megalithic building going on.

Please understand us here; we're not saying these societies were or are of less value, or "not as good" as the technological one which dominates the world today. On the contrary, they were rich in many ways, had wonderful spiritual values among many other things, and knew much we did not, including how to better survive in their regions.

The early white settlers of Massachusetts would not have survived their first winter, if it hadn't been for the timely help of the Native Americans, for instance. They knew how to survive. More importantly, this stress on survival included avoiding wasting time and effort building what to them would have been useless monumental structures—smart people that they were!

Our point here is that people who function at a primitive subsistence level today, do not build monumental megaliths. So why their ancestors and ours would have done such around the world 10,000 years ago would seem unlikely, unless they were coerced or forced to do this. They simply didn't have the spare "capital" to expend on such massive endeavors, unless made to do so.

After all, Malthus,[103] a definitive researcher on the subject of population, tells us that there were natural checks on the levels populations could reach. These included premature death from starvation and disease, wars over scarce resources, etc. These all lead, inevitably, to a "Malthusian" type of catastrophe, which acts to collapse and plunge the population back to a "sustainable" level.

For example, if those ancient people overindulged in their hunting capabilities and wiped out all the game in any given area, they'd subsequently starve, or they'd have to move on. If they didn't, there would be a dieback, and the population then would shrink. A lack of game meant a lack of food, which in turn meant death from starvation and disease.[104] This resulted in their constantly being on the move as they hunted or fished out a given area.

Yet, they had an overwhelming need to build massive stone structures that served them no immediate purpose, and when life was so very precarious for them already. Really? Really? We don't think so.

We need to drive this point home some more. As an analogy of just how serious this would be, picture yourself suddenly lost in the mountains, in woods, and you know the weather is going to turn bitterly cold (remember, this is back before the glaciers completely retreated in the last Ice Age). Would you try to find water, food, and build a shelter for yourself, or would you instead pile blocks of stones together to make a seemingly pointless platform to please God or some gods?

Well, that's exactly what mainstream archaeologists are asking us to believe those people did, that they were that stupid. We wouldn't be here today if our ancestors were that pathetic when it came to wanting to survive. No, it just isn't logical at all.

Building such things wasn't our ancestors' only task. One of the enterprises they seemed to have been involved with, when they weren't too busy carving and moving all those giant blocks for everything, seems to have been mining. They dug various ores from the earth around those ancient dates, and even much earlier, it seems.

Of course, the one ore we're all thinking about here is the most obvious one of all, gold. Gold seems to have been high on the list of priorities for the rulers of Megalithia. How do we know this? Moreover, how do we know this isn't all just supposition, people making wild guesses, stabs in the dark, as it were, about this idea of mining?

Well, again we have to fall back on whatever available evidence we can find. We can look for physical evidence of such mining activities and try to date them. We can also look at stories, historical records, legends, and myths that might talk about this, as well.

After all, many different groups of people handed down verbal histories, and often as we've discovered recently, they were quite accurate. We in the West did the same thing until we discovered writing, even as those earlier peoples did.

Of course, no one legend would suffice under such conditions. There would have to be independent corroboration by other tales of other cultures to help substantiate the truthfulness of such things, or at least their likelihood of being true. Nevertheless, if you have enough such legends that say much the same thing, and they come from different civilizations scattered around the globe, then you may consider that there is some real substance, some truth to them.

For instance, almost every culture in the world seems to have some version of the Great Flood tale. Whether we're talking the Middle East, North America, Africa, Australia or Asia, this is so. Now scholars and scientists are beginning to think there may well have been such an event, and are even actively researching the idea fully these days. Whereas, once they just took it to be "just a myth."

So let's do the same thing, try to find evidence through such means to support our contention about mining. We'll start with what we in the West call myths, and what those in the Middle East and Far East call their history.

**The Ancient Sumerians' Anunnaki and Gold Mining:** Zecharia Sitchin,[105] an author who taught himself how to read Sumerian cuneiform, has made some bold statements, ones which he backs up by referring to the writings on the clay tablets of the ancient Sumerians. This writing is in "cuneiform."

According to him and Sumerian history, and they did think of it as their history and not just as legends, a race of beings from the sky came to Earth. These beings called themselves the Anunnaki or "Sky Guardians," and they had marvelous powers, one of which was the ability to fly around in machines.

As a very strange and curious side note, the Old Testament of the Bible, and the Hebrew Torah from which that Testament was drawn, mention a race of giants that sound remarkably similar to the Anunnaki. Where the Anunnaki were a race of demigods from the skies who were powerful and strong, as well as long-lived, as the Sumerians state, the Bible refers to the Nephilim as:[106]

> *"The Nephilim were on the earth in those days,*
> *and also afterward, when the sons of God came in to the*
> *daughters of man and they bore children to them. These*
> *were the mighty men who were of old, the men of renown."*

**—Genesis 6:4**

Here, the Bible is referring to many of the greatest known (biblical) offspring of the Nephilim and humans. One attribute of these hybrid children seems to have been incredible longevity. Gilgamesh, the hero of the famous epic of the same name, was also known as "Nimrod." He was supposedly the offspring of the Anunnaki.

The Nephilim also came down from the sky, just as the Anunnaki did. No, it doesn't stop there! Many cultures have legends of the gods or even God interbreeding with humans. Hercules[107] was an offspring of the Greek Gods, for instance. Even in Christianity, Mary is said to have given birth to Jesus after an "immaculate conception."

Ancient Egyptian religion contains similar stories, as do the Old Norse religions. Odin or "Woten" was said to come to Earth in disguise to breed with human women. Native tribes of the American Southwest also have stories of the "sky people" or "star people" that came to Earth and impregnated women.[108]

The name, "Anunnaki," means "those who Anu sent from heaven to earth." Nephilim means, "to fall down to Earth, to land" (at the "Landing Place," as Baalbek was known?). Eloheem[109] (which beings figure prominently in the story of Jacob's Ladder, "gods were revealed," source: Genesis 35:7) and "Eloheem" come from the Torah and means "these Beings."

In an ancient dialect of Arabic, they used the name "Jabaariyn,"[110] which means "the mighty ones," or possibly "majestic ones." In Aramaic Hebrew, the term "Gibborim" was used. It means "the might ones," as well. Finally, in Egyptian, the term, "Neteru"[111] was the one they used when referring to beings similar to the Anunnaki.

Now, are all these comparable stories just the result of mere coincidences? It stretches one's credulity to believe this. One or two might be termed a coincidence, but not when there are this many, and they are worldwide.

Please note: The fact that stories of the Great Flood and that every culture seems to have a version of it, means that somehow, everyone, worldwide, was affected by something, some sort of deluge. The same must hold true, then, in this case with "sky guardians," "star people," "sky gods," or whatever name was used for them around the globe.

If cultures worldwide have creation stories and myths concerning beings from the sky coming down, powerful or "mighty" ones who were like gods and chose at times to breed with humans, and cause famous and potent offspring to be born, then there must be something to this "myth," as well. Whatever these beings were, they seem to have affected the world as a whole. They left powerful stories about themselves that have echoed down through the millennia. This lends further credence to the idea Megalithia was a worldwide empire and that such beings may have actually existed. The stories of them are just too prolific to ignore.

In any case, the Anunnaki in particular, seemed to have had a predilection for gold.[112] They wanted it. They needed it. What's more, they demanded it. When it came to the desire for gold, they were just as greedy as any human was, or perhaps more. Of course, they claimed they wanted it to help their home world to survive, to help rejuvenate their atmosphere.[113] Possibly, but who really knows?

Moreover, they wanted it so badly that the Sumerians say they created the human race (us) just to mine the gold for them, because they hated doing the job themselves. In other words, they wanted homegrown slaves who could work well on Planet Earth, because they were native to it, and who would save them a lot of exertion and trouble on their own part in obtaining the precious metal.

Lucky them! However, not so lucky for humanity, if this is true, because it means we were a race born to be slaves. No, to put it more bluntly, we weren't born to slavery; we were created to be a slave race as a species. It would explain why there could be interbreeding between our species and at least one of theirs, if this is true. We may share DNA.

Moreover, for all our troubles, we were also supposed to worship and revere the Anunnaki as gods and faithfully to serve them in all their needs. To say the least, this is adding insult to injury. Oh well! Such is the lot of slaves, it seems.

Nevertheless, from earliest times, we have legends (histories?) with regard to cruel rulers from the sky, wanting Earth's gold and forcing us to get it for them. As always, there's more.

In the New World, various native tribes refer to gods from

the sky that had a penchant for their gold, as well. The natives would appease this demand by making offerings of gold. Rumors have abounded for centuries of lost cities of gold in the New World. Eldorado is a good example. The Seven Golden Cities of Cibola is another.

In addition, attendant with these stories of places of gold, are rumors of sky creatures, legends of sky gods, sky guardians, star people, call them what you will, and this even includes the god, Quetzalcoatl, who came to the New World by flight. He is also known as the "Feathered Serpent." He figures prominently in a number of Central American civilizations, including the Mayan and Aztec, as well as other Mesoamerican civilizations.[114] As an additional side note, the Anunnaki were depicted with feathered wings in ancient drawings of them.[115]

So a worldwide link between gold and perhaps an alien (or aliens) ruling class, such as the Anunnaki, seems to be a recurring theme. Legends around the globe seem to abound with such ideas. In fact, gold has always been strongly linked to the eternal and the supernatural. This is why, today, we still use it for wedding rings, to symbolize our eternal love and bond when married.

Now, is there actual evidence of such mining operations from so long ago? Yes, it would seem there is. Here are a few examples:

**Ancient Gold Mines in South Africa:** Sumerian cuneiform records refer to Abzu a city founded by the Anunnaki god (so-called) by the name of Enki. This particular member of the Anunnaki, by the way, is also supposed to have been the one who created humanity and who founded the first city, Eridu.[116] The city of Abzu (or ABZU,[117] depending on what source one uses), was supposed to have been below the equator, on the continent of Africa.

Yes, this is the stuff of legends again, but recently, something very extraordinary has become known. An ancient ruin of a city in South Africa, one that is said to have over one hundred thousand stone ruins, does exist.[118] This, according to the researchers involved, was no small metropolis! It was located over a wide geographic area and included such sites as modern-day Carolina, Badplaas, Waterval, and Machadodorp.

Just who built the place or why, is at present, unknown. However, it had everything a city was supposed to have, including roads, houses, religious sites—you name it—it appears to have had it. Many postulate this city is from where the Anunnaki "god," Enki, directed his mining operations. Others claim Solomon may have built it, because he, too, was said to have access to a mine in Africa.

There's evidence of ancient gold mining all over the region, as well. Some estimates place the earliest such mines at close to 250,000 years ago! Others say some are 50,000 years old, and still others say the mining took place around 10,000 to 25,000 years ago.[119] Again, we have a timeframe that includes the time of Megalithia.

Michael Tellinger,[120] a scientist, even proposes a far-reaching idea that the stone circles found in the region were used as part of a massive power grid. It is his theory that somehow, the ancients were able to create some form of energy with them. Whether this was propagated as frequencies of sound or some other means, such as resonating methods, is unclear, but various persons have suggested all these methods.

However, it is Michael's contention this energy (whatever it was) was then used to help to mine gold. Perhaps this is an idea even too radical for us seriously to entertain, but the fact there are extensive ruins there is incontrovertible. The age of them is another cause of disagreement—as always with matters pertaining to stone structures, but some argue the city itself is as much as 160,000 years old! If this is true, it's extraordinary.

Michael Tellinger even thinks such civilizations may well have dated back 212,000 years ago or more. He points to Sumerian records of the times of their kings' reigns to prove his point, among other sources. Therefore, Megalithia could well have been around a very long time before it fell, even longer than we suspect. If so, it was an incredibly stable regime. Then, we've already mentioned how it was designed to be static, to maintain long-term control of the populace. Perhaps, it was more stable than we think.

Then there is the matter of this mysterious energy? Is it possible it has to do with, or that they somehow drew or concentrated it from ley lines? Again, we cannot entirely discount this idea, because we simply don't know. For all we do know, it might be that the mysterious Dark Energy scientists now speak of, was the power source. Reputable scientists today say it might be possible to harness Dark Energy. Perhaps, the Anunnaki had discovered how.

Whatever the truth is there, this does seem to be a recurring theme throughout all of this, this idea of a mysterious energy[121] and it having something to do with ley lines. Whether we're discussing the possible real purposes of the Egyptian pyramids, the ley lines in Europe, or the gold mines of South Africa, this idea keeps popping up to haunt us, this concept of an unknown energy whose secret we've lost over the ages, or perhaps we humans never knew in the first place. Might it have been a secret reserved to the "sky gods" alone and one we humans were never privy to?

Moreover, of course, as we clearly have already admitted, there is controversy over the age and purpose of the ruins in South Africa. There always is. There is even better evidence for a 50,000-year-old gold mine.[122] In addition, it's not the only one. Ancient gold mines seem to number in the hundreds, perhaps even thousands.

Now remember, all this was supposedly going on at a time when archaeologists tell us that humans didn't use any kind of metals at all. They were simply using stone tools. So just how would such primitives mine gold? Where did they find the time when they were supposed to be hunter-gatherers? More to the point, how did they even know gold existed? How would they have been able to smelt it if they had?

There are more questions. For instance, why would such extraordinarily primitive people bother to mine gold? We see no evidence of pieces of jewelry or other items dating from those extremely ancient times. We see no tools made of the substance.

So where did the gold they mined go? Who was using it, if not them?

The Sumerians say the answer is with the Anunnaki. They wanted the gold and they took it off world, supposedly because their planet's atmosphere needed rejuvenation and gold was a necessary part of the process. Yet, apparently, they didn't just want gold. Their prehistoric mines were for accumulating other sorts of ores and minerals for them, as well. These include copper, tin, hematite, quartz, and iron. Even coal was mined. Here are just some examples of this sort of thing:

**Wattis, Utah Coal Mine 1953:** We mentioned this in another of our books, because it is just so intriguing. While excavating a new tunnel at the Lion Coal Mine, miners discovered an already existing mine when they broke through into one of its tunnels. However, they discovered something very strange about this mine. It was old! So old was the exposed coal in the newly revealed tunnels, so weathered was it that it wouldn't even burn, it was that ancient!

Two professors, Drs. Wilson and Jennings, both from the University of Utah found not only incredibly long tunnels (one was well over a mile in length and never fully explored), but even special storage places where mined coal was accumulated prior to being removed from the mine. The native tribes of North America never historically used coal, ever, as far as archaeologists can determine, let alone mine it. So it begs the question, just who did use this coal and just how long ago? We think the answer lies with the Empire of Megalithia.

**Iron Mine in Ngwenya, Africa:** 1967, and iron miners discovered already existing tunnels, ancient ones branching off from their own, just as with the Lion Coal Mine. These ancient tunnels dated as far back as 40,000 B.C.E. As if that isn't bizarre enough, apparently, over 100,000 tons of ore has already been removed from those tunnels during the time they'd been actively mined. That's a lot of ore! This was no minor operation, with just a few primitives picking around for bits and pieces of ore.

Mind you, this was tens of thousands of years before the

Iron Age came into being. Who was using so much iron at a time when everyone was supposed to have been using strictly stone, if even that? Again, we think it might've been under the auspices of Megalithia this mining went on, for the dates put it well back into the time of the Megalithian Empire.

**Band of Holes in Pisco Valley, Peru:**[123] Anyone enjoy looking at holes? Well, if you do, we recommend the Pisco Valley in Peru. This extremely arid region is home to the famous, or perhaps "infamous" would be a better way of phrasing it, Band of Holes. There are literally thousands of these holes dug, or in many cases, carved into the raw rock and hard dry soil there.

Just how many holes? Well, one source says there are approximately 6,900 such holes![124] The Band of Holes is about 66 feet wide (and yes, it seems to be a very regular width), and runs for about a mile. The holes are regularly spaced. The average depth was from seven to three feet deep.

Moreover, the holes are old! Aerial views show old dry watercourses cutting through the area, right across them, having destroyed some of the holes in the process. When one considers that often the area gets *no rainfall at all for years at a time* this shows how slow the erosion process is in that region. In other words, these holes have been there a very long time for such washed away portions to occur to such a degree.

What is the purpose of the holes? We have no idea. That they regularly repeated themselves, are quite close together, and so form a band that marches in a ribbon across the barren landscape is there for anyone to see. What are they? Again, nobody knows. This is yet another case of a great deal of effort being expended by someone in a hostile arid region and for a totally unknown purpose.

Perhaps they are test holes, such as engineers create when checking for minerals and resources in a given area. Then if this is so, why are there so very many of them, and so closely packed together? The sheer number of them simply shouldn't be necessary. Much more widely spaced holes would accomplish the same thing and not nearly so many would have been needed.

There is an almost robotic sameness, a monotonous repetitiveness to the holes that gives one a feeling some automated process must have created them. Some say they may have been used for burials, but such a notion is absurd. No bone fragments, let alone bones, or other funeral-related artifacts have ever been found there, not one.

Others suggested they were for grain storage. This seems the most ludicrous idea of all. Why go to such extreme measures to store grain in the middle of nowhere, when there are much easier methods? In addition, exactly how was the grain stored? What type of containers or at least lids was used to cover the holes? Where are they? No trace of such has ever been found, and neither has any leftover grain been discovered, not any, not even a few grains. In addition, who in their right mind would store it in such a manner anyway?

We know that for humans to have created them by hand, would have been a major and massive undertaking, and on the face of it, a seemingly totally useless one. The holes are much too shallow to have been attempts at finding water. Nothing of any sorts seems to have been buried in them. Therefore, the reason for their existence is a mystery, and an old one. Just how old is hard to say, but again, if one goes by the erosion patterns that have since developed, they are very old!

There is still more to discuss here about ancient Megalithia. There seems to have been other types of industry, as well. One of these, oddly, seems to have been the production of hi-tech screws. Yes, we said screws. Here's why:

**Thousands of Spiral Shaped Objects "Screws" Found in Ural Mountains of Russia:**[125] We mentioned this topic in another of our books, as well, and we mention it here, because this is an odd coincidence. This discovery was made while people were prospecting for gold, no less, in the Ural Mountains. Again, that annoying gold connection rears its head.

In any case, thousands of screw-like objects have been discovered. The first findings were made in the early 1990s. They have continued on and off since then.

Buried in layers of earth anywhere from just three feet in depth to as much as 40 feet, these objects are thought to be about 20,000 years old. The objects, which range in size from as much as a little over an inch to less than 1/1,000 of an inch (virtually nano-sized), seem to be made of many different types of metals. These include some extremely rare ones, such as titanium and tungsten. The smelting of some of these metals requires extremely high temperatures. We have achieved some of these necessary temperatures ourselves only as recently as the Twentieth Century.

So who made these "screw-like" objects? Why did they? What purpose did they serve? How did they all end up buried where they are, in the middle of nowhere? Remember, we're talking about thousands of them here, in different sizes, and composed of different metals and alloys. Moreover, they were scattered over a wide region.

If this is some sort of a hoax, it is a very elaborate one, indeed. What's more, it would have been very hard to do, since we simply don't manufacture such items. The cost of the metal alone would be one detriment. The temperatures required would be another. Added to this, the sheer number of different types and sizes of the screws would make a very difficult hoax to perpetrate, indeed, if not impossible.

Finally, we have to ask, what would be the point? Why go to such elaborate and expensive lengths to create such a pointless hoax. Don't forget, they had to bury these screws all over the place, even down to forty feet deep! They had to do this without disturbing the area, so that it looked as if they'd been naturally buried over time there.

No signs of digging could show. Somehow, they had to do this without disturbing the layers of soil and earth around the screws. Again, we're not talking just a few screws here. We're talking thousands found along one river and a tributary of it some miles away.

No, this is no hoax. What it does show is someone had some type of advanced industry a very long time ago. It was an industry that used metals and alloys, some of which we've only recently begun to use ourselves, and only very recently.

Besides thousands of buried high-tech "screws," researchers have also found some evidence of terraforming. Terraforming is the reshaping of a planet's surface on a grand scale. Here's some information we've discovered posted in the Pravda Newspaper of Russia. Pravda has long been considered *the* source for news in that country. It was the official organ of the government under the old Soviet Union.

**The Map of "the Creator" or the Dashka Stone:**[126] A "great plate" was discovered in 1999. As we mentioned in another book, scientists at the Bashkir University claim this plate (made of stone and huge in size) constitutes (according to them) incontrovertible proof that there once was an ancient and advanced civilization.

The plate shows a bas-relief map, a surprisingly three-dimensional one. It is equal to many such types of military maps today in many ways. The depiction is of the region's River along with its adjacent tributaries. The map appears to show great engineering feats, including water channels no less than 1,200 km long. Also included are a system of weirs, canals, and large dams.

There appears to be a written language on the map, as well. At first thought to be an older, ancient form of Chinese, it has since been determined the language is completely unknown. An interesting aspect of this Map of the Creator is that it appears to have been done from an aerial vantage point, at least tens of thousands of feet high. Moreover, the three-dimensional quality is impressive, even by today's standards.

It is also believed this map is a piece of a much larger one. According to Russian archives, during the seventeenth and eighteenth centuries, researchers of the Ural Mountains area claim to have seen some two hundred slabs of stone just like this one.

Furthermore, the map itself is not on the very surface of the stone but seems to be under a protective clear layer of substance, and then backed by another type, thus forming a sort of stone sandwich. Dolomite forms the base. The second level, with the map itself, is made of diopside glas. How it was treated is unknown. The final layer is a two-millimeter thick sheath of transparent calcium-porcelain. Again, this is apparently to protect the surface of the map from damage. How these layers were bonded together is another mystery.

This one piece of a much greater map is large in its own right, "It is 148 centimeters high, 106 centimeters wide, and 16 centimeters thick."[127] So large is the Map of the Creator, that the estimated weight of it is one ton. Special wooden rollers had to be made to move the object. In addition, the map is to scale. It has a ratio of 1:1.1 kilometers. There are definitely megalithic qualities about the map, considering its large size, being made of stone, etc.

Again, this simply can't be a hoax. For someone to recreate this map in stone and in such a huge piece of stone at that, would seem to be a ridiculous notion. What's more, we don't know how it was done. Add to this, the map is an aerial view. It maintains a good ratio, which is kept throughout the mapping process, and doesn't vary. In other words, it's a very accurate, three-dimensional map of the region. If this were a deception, we would love to meet the hoaxer(s), for he/she/they would have to be geniuses.

Now for a final point about the Map of the Creator, the map is old, very old. It could be as much as one hundred and twenty million years old! It does depict the Ufa River region in detail. In addition, it would seem to show the river had been deliberately diverted to its present day course along with the creation of all those dams, weirs, and canals (now long gone). Interesting, isn't it?

Was someone actually moving rivers around 120 million years ago? If so, who? Why? Of course, the map may not be that old. Our same old problem rears its head here. It is very hard to determine the age of things composed of rock. However, that it predates the beginnings of our civilization would seem to be a certainty.

**Chapter Conclusion:** There unquestionably seems to have

been evidence for quite a bit of mining and other industry during the time span of Megalithia. Ancient clay tablets refer to it. Legends from the Old and the New World mention this topic repeatedly. Discoveries of a prehistoric city near the ancient goldmines of South Africa provide extra support for this idea.

Truly ancient goldmines, as well as an incredibly old coalmine in northern Utah, along with long-abandoned iron, hematite, quartz, and other types of mines, would all seem to indicate the mining industry was alive and well at a time when no one was supposed even to be even using any metals at all. According to mainstream archaeologists, not only weren't they using such ores, but they didn't know such minerals even existed. Apparently, the alien rulers of Megalithia did.

One last thing in this regard and that is we simply cannot account for The Map of the Creator. It is truly a unique object. However, despite determining its age being so difficult, we include it here, since it would seem to be an example of the same sort of megalithic style of artisanship, being made of stone. We don't even know how the thing was made!

We do know it's very old, so old, it either falls into the time of the Megalithia Empire, or perhaps even earlier. Is this yet another tantalizing sign that Megalithia was an incredibly stable civilization and may have existed in a stable state for tens, even hundreds of thousands of years? Again, we simply don't know, but this is provocative evidence this may have been so.

Regardless of age, the Map of the Creator makes for strong evidence for our case that there was a highly advanced civilization long before our own came into being. In the case of the Map of the Creator, it may have been very long ago, indeed.

# PART 4
# WHAT WAS MEGALITHIA LIKE?

# Chapter 10

## The Society and Size of Megalithia

As we've mentioned earlier, the total population of the world at the time of Megalithia's existence, was not large. We mention it again here, because this had a huge impact on the type of society Megalithia probably had. By today's standards, the entire populace only amounted to that of a small country of today. Therefore, Megalithia certainly did not have a huge population or the resources in the terms of labor that would usually go with such.

Because of the small size of the population, the evidence that the Empire was worldwide, we believe for this reason and others that the Megalithian Empire must have consisted mostly of small towns and settlements, and these were widely scattered about, placed where they were of the most use to the overlords of Megalithia.

Therefore, although the Empire encompassed the entire globe, its actual areas of direct control were probably severely limited. In addition, as we mentioned in our overview of Megalithia, those settlements and villages probably were mostly coastal in their locations, but with notable exceptions.

There were settlements inland, as well, such as near mining operations. The means of communication and travel amongst the settlements was probably minimal. Our belief is that transportation and communication was done almost entirely through the auspices of the ruling class, because of their ability to fly using their machines. The alternative would have been by primitive boats created by humans.

Since the horse had not yet been domesticated for human use, and probably few other animals, as well, such as oxen, the choices seem to have been to either walk, go by boat, or as a rare passenger aboard one of the aliens' airships. Remember, we're talking so far back in time that even cats, and probably dogs, weren't pets of humans yet, let alone horses, cattle, and the rest.

What did this mean for the average citizen of Megalithia? Well, first, it meant they were highly isolated most of the time and relegated to small communities, most of which were no more than villages or mere hamlets. Most citizens of Megalithia probably didn't travel much at all. We estimate that the average person living at the time probably went no more than three to seven miles away from their home during their entire lifetime. We formulated this limit based on how far they could walk and return in one day.

Although Megalithia was an empire, its citizens wouldn't have seen it as such. The average person lived an insulated and isolated existence, they, and their few neighbors. Their contact with the "outside" world would've been only through their overlords, or their overlords' direct minions.

In this regard, "minion" might refer to a puppet king or prince acting on behalf of the true ruling class, or even the human servants, the priesthood to the aliens. Many of these isolated communities might not even have been aware of others, or just how wide the rule of the aliens extended, so cut off from the rest of the world, were they. Theirs would have been more of a relationship with their overlords then their fellow human settlements.

The population of Megalithia was probably little better off than that of actual slaves. Except for those who directly served their overlords, those creatures from another world, life must have been dismal. No doubt, it was often monotonous and harsh, as well.

According to the Sumerian cuneiform writings, humans

worked in the mines for their masters. Undoubtedly, they also aided in manufacturing and making those things the masters wished to have, whether a temple/palace, or furnishings for it, etc. Some probably produced food for their masters' consumption. Because of the small population and therefore small labor pool, it is likely humans worked constantly at hard and dirty tasks. This would have been a miserable existence by most people's standards of today.

Why do we arrive at this conclusion? Because the Sumerians' beliefs in an afterlife were of a thoroughly miserable one. Upon dying, one was relegated to a gray and dirty world. They ate ashes. It was not a happy afterlife or one to look forward to! However, it does show how downtrodden these inhabitants of Megalithia must have been, so oppressed that not even the afterlife offered them any hope of bettering their lot.

However, this does point out an inherent weakness of the Empire. Although ruling classes are rarely, if ever truly overthrown by their slaves, despite what we see in movies and read in popular fiction, rebellions, or a grand rebellion, probably did occur at some point in Megalithia. This is because the ruling class, although immensely powerful, appears to have been few in numbers. They literally couldn't be everywhere at once. Control was thus difficult to maintain. Maintaining their authority must have been a slippery business. Often, it would seem they used human armies to help them in their battles, according to the ancient Vedic texts of India.[128]

Therefore, it would have been reasonably easy for isolated populations to go "native" and simply melt away into the still-endless woods that existed at the time, or to flee onto the plains, savannahs, or off into the rugged mountains.[129] Many probably did just that. We can only imagine how dire the consequences would be if these runaways were ever caught.

Nevertheless, for all their supremacy, the rule of the masters of Megalithia must've been an uneasy one at the best of times. Yet, they did have immense power on their side and that was their incredible technology. With it, they probably managed to maintain reasonable control. They did this until some greater event eventually occurred to upset that stability.

For a more modern-day comparison of what the Empire of Megalithia may have been like, think of the British Empire. Despite it having an excellent fleet of ships, locomotives, the use of the telegraph, and even the telephone in the final days of the Empire, not to mention huge armies, the rule of the British was an uneasy one almost all the time.

They always were at war, it seems. They fought all sorts of enemies, ones who wished to take their possessions away from them. Alternatively, they were busy quelling rebellions in unruly provinces and/or colonies that wanted their freedom, ones that pushed to throw off the British yoke of rule. The American Revolution is an early example of this. There have been many others.

The Great Mutiny in India is yet another instance of rebellion against the English mother country. Then there are the wars these rebellions triggered, helped to cause, or resulted from, such as the battle for the control of the Sudan, the Crimean War, the Boer War, World War I, and even World War II. At the time of the American Revolution, England was also at war with France, the Netherlands, and Spain, along with their upstart American colonies, a virtual world war of the times.

For the rulers of Megalithia, it must have been even more difficult to maintain control. Faced with highly scattered and isolated populations, tiny ones, and an inability or desire constantly to exercise direct control over them, and being small in numbers themselves, they must've had a tough time of it.

Mind you, one doesn't feel sorry for them. If the stories about the Anunnaki are true, they were a vicious and brutal lot. They went to any lengths to seize power and to keep it.

The same seems to be true of the stories told about the alien rulers in the ancient books of India, the Ramayana,[130] and the Mahabharata.[131] The control of the populations by the masters was absolute whenever they could manage it, and dissension was never tolerated. They ruled with an iron fist (if they had fists), and backed this up with weapons of mass destruction. These texts also speak of rebellions and/or internal conflicts, as well.

If all this wasn't hard enough on our poor alien masters (this is sarcasm here), there are the problems they had with each other. In both the Sumerian cuneiform texts, as well as in the Vedic texts, there is much written about the masters having disagreements with each other, conflicts of a minor sort, as well as those of major proportions.

Even other belief systems around the world speak of the same thing. The Norse peoples speak of Ragnarok,[132] the end of the world and doom of the gods" from which the Germans get Gotterdammerung, or the "Twilight of the Gods." The gods of the Greeks, those that resided on Mt. Olympus, fought not only their forebears, the Titans, but also each other in raging battles, often using humans as pawns, as well. So it goes and continues to go. There is a worldwide mythos, or perhaps distorted history of those ancient aliens, what they may have done at the dawn of history.

Here again is yet more evidence in the form of such global legends that helps support the contention of such a ruling class of Megalithia. One or two such similar tales of gods warring like this from different cultures would be coincidence. But when so many, scattered so widely around the world, all say much the same thing, some common root, some true account must be the basis of all those tales, however distorted they've become over time.

We feel it likely there is a sort of subconscious "racial memory" of the aliens in this respect, one handed down through verbal means over countless generations. That racial memory speaks of them as gods of one sort or another. Those legends also speak of bizarre creatures, as well.

We also think the level of conflict in the Empire gradually rose, until it reached a crescendo that was catastrophic in its nature, and we mean catastrophic! In the Vedic texts, there is even talk of a major war, one on a truly cosmic scale, literally. We will discuss these stories later on, in the chapter concerning the final days of Megalithia and its ultimate downfall.

Another thing; the coastal nature of the settlements of much of Megalithia also was a major weakness. If anything should happen to those, the Empire would face ruin. What trade and/or commerce there was, that which was maintained by shipping instead of by air, would end if there were no port cities to receive the goods or ship them. We think this trade did come to an abrupt end. We feel certain there was coastal flooding around the world. This is when the many legends of various drowned cities were born. Again, we will discuss this in more depth later on.

Although Megalithia claimed the entire world as its empire, we now know it wasn't the type of empire that we think of today. With small isolated populations, as well as many nomadic ones, the ruling class had to be ruthless in order to keep charge of it all. With the primitive nature of its citizens, who used only stone implements and tools at best, the only real technology was that belonging to the ruling class itself.

It appears instead of having one "emperor," those that ruled were more likely a type of oligarchy, with those powerful creatures vying for control and dominance over each other and various regions of the planet. In that respect, Megalithia was probably much like the Roman Empire. Still, there is a difference. The rulers of the Roman Empire were human. We think the rulers of Megalithia were extraterrestrials. The evidence would seem to support our contention.

**Chapter Conclusion:** Now to summarize; we have given you an overview of Megalithian society and its structure. We have cited examples of the nature of the massive platforms that were built during this time, and which help to give us a timeframe for Megalithia, itself. We have discussed its other types of architecture, and that which was reserved for the subjugated peoples, how primitive it was by comparison.

We have shown this was a real dichotomy in that civilization, with the ruling class demanding and getting massive structures of stone, while the human citizens of Megalithia probably had to settle for mud huts or something very similar.

We have also discussed several of the types of industries Megalithia may have had. Among these were mining, production of some foodstuffs, and apparently, there was even manufacturing of a sort. Again, there is a real dichotomy going on here in that society. While the mass of Megalithia's citizens eked out a subsistence-level existence and worked for their masters, the aliens had the sole benefit of the mining operations and the manufacturing (spiral screws, as one example).

All this was strictly for the use and the purposes of the ruling class. We have no evidence at all to support the idea that the populace, in general, had access to these sorts of things for their own use.

One more time, if this seems like an alien idea to you (pun intended), look again to Mother England, or "Old Blimey," as its expatriates, those who went to the colonies to make their fortunes, sometimes affectionately or otherwise, referred to the country.

You see, the English did much the same thing as the aliens. They even had a name for it. They called it Mercantilism. Remember that this was the notion the colonies existed for the good of the mother country. So the idea the aliens might practice this same thing with us, is it really so far-fetched a concept when we, ourselves, also invented it, and not so very long ago?

# Chapter 11

## Who Was the Ruling Class of Megalithia?

Now we come to one of the most critical parts of our theory about the Empire of Megalithia, and that is the nature of the ruling class, itself. We've already made it clear we think they were alien in nature, literally, being extraterrestrials from another world, or worlds. Moreover, based on the Vedas of India, the Mahabharata and the Ramayana, as well as the cuneiform writings about the Anunnaki, it would seem the ruling class was divided amongst themselves. Although they all may have been equals with each other, they were not necessarily on good terms at all.

In the Sumerian texts, they talk of rivalries and conflicts between the rulers. They also talk about open clashes, skirmishes, and battles. The Anunnaki, according to the Sumerian texts, were clearly beings from another world. The texts say exactly this. They even describe the home world, and name it, Niburu.[133]

The Vedic texts refer to beings from other worlds, as well, and how they fought each other. According to those same texts, it appears our world may have been a real cause of disagreement among these alien species. We may have been a colony world in an interstellar border zone between space territories occupied different extraterrestrials

In fact, legends and myths from around the world, oral histories, and written texts, describe beings from the sky that fought each other. For instance:

**The Dogon People:**[134] We've mentioned these people in another book for much the same reason. The Dogon are a tribe in Africa, and they believed strange beings came from the star system of Sirius B. Sirius A is a star, the brightest in the heavens.

However and strangely, the Dogon knew of the companion star, Sirius B. We didn't know about that star until the mid-twentieth century. We couldn't see it, not even with telescopes of the day. So how did the Dogon people of Africa know about it? Yet, their entire religion is based on just that. They perform ceremonies of an elaborate nature, in elaborate and weird costumes, simulating how the creatures looked.

Entire books have been written on the subject. We are talking tomes worthy of professional researchers and scientists, ones that for laypeople are hard to follow. Although some scientists refute the work of the two original scientists/researchers who did the study among the Dogon people, both those original researchers adamantly stand by their findings. They claim there was no inadvertent pollution of the Dogon beliefs by them. They declare that rigorous standards were followed in their research techniques.

This is a typical reaction of western researchers and scientists when something like this is discovered. If you can't refute the results on their own lack of merit, then question the means by which they were obtained. If all else fails, question the veracity of the researchers themselves in order to discredit their results, even if they are Westerners, too.

Worse, in the process, these detractors aren't just destroying the professional reputations of their colleagues by doing this, but are also being condescending to the Dogon People in thinking their religion, an ancient one, could be so easily changed by a couple of researchers just making inquiries into it. This is tantamount to saying the Dogon are inferior to us. After all, would a couple of people inquiring about Catholicism, as an example, cause the Church to change its stance on whom and what Jesus was? Not hardly! However, apparently, so-called "primitive" people are much more easily swayed compared to us? How condescending an idea.

Whether the Hopi Indians, the ancient Egyptians who claimed their first rulers were sky guardians, or the history of the Anunnaki, the Mayans with their deities from the sky, or India with their alien rulers, everything seems to point towards beings from the sky coming to our Earth, dominating us, and having conflicts among themselves and perhaps with us.

Again, lest you dismiss this as just the idle superstitions of uneducated and primitive peoples, we must point out the following: even our Western beliefs of Christianity, Muslim, and Jewish faiths, all believe in a God in the heavens. They also believe He sent heavenly messengers to earth on a regular basis. They further all believe that on occasion, humans of Earth were taken up into heaven. We leave you to judge. Is just about everybody on the planet, all other histories, whether oral or written, whether called legends or myths, wrong, even when the tenets of our "superior" faiths agree in many instances with them?

Alternatively, is there some truth to all this? We believe there is and a lot of it. The stories and beliefs are just too widespread, certainly too endemic worldwide, and too prevalent just to disregard, to dismiss out of hand as mere myths and legends.

So what would these alien rulers actually be like? There has been a tremendous amount of discussion about this topic. The television show, *Ancient Aliens*, is just one of many examples of this passion to know more about ancient aliens.

So again, what do we know? Well, by all accounts, we know there were definite class distinctions between "them" and "us." The Anunnaki, in particular, seem to have been this way. We can't say for sure, but we suspect that genetic manipulation is very much a part of the practices they performed on humanity.

We say this, because several sources recount similar such concepts. Egyptian religion abounds with depictions of creatures that are half-human and half something else. The early pharaohs of Egypt were said to have elongated heads. The Pharaoh, Akhenaten, is actually depicted as having one. In addition, sarcophagi have been found, huge ones, which contain smashed bones. One, a monstrous sarcophagus, contains smashed bones mixed in with some type of black, tar-like, sticky substance.

Egyptologists claim the Serapeum tomb at Saqqara was for a cult that venerated bulls. Not likely. No bull's skeletal remains were ever found there. Yes, some were found near Alexandria, but those were created much later in the time of the Romans, when the belief in Mithras (with a sacred bull as the central symbol) was popular, but this was thousands of years later.

So what was buried at Saqqara, if not a bull? What was interned in such a way so that it could never come forth again? Someone went through great trouble to entomb whatever it was in a way that it could never revive, with a lid placed on the remains that would take a giant to lift![135]

This tells us something about the nature of whatever it was, if only vaguely. We can reasonably surmise that whatever it was, they considered it dangerous, powerful, and an abomination to be so interred in such a manner. So frightened were those who buried it, that they went to extraordinary lengths to make sure it never came back to haunt their lives again, couldn't escape the confines of its giant sarcophagus.

So just what was so important to bury so that it could never escape again, or come back to life? Something hideous, no doubt, and something that frightened the Egyptians of the time out of their wits.

The Egyptians weren't alone in showing hybrid humans and animals. The Sumerians, for example, show similar hybrid creatures in their depictions. So do many other cultures around the world, along with images of fantastic creatures, whether dragons, griffins, or whatever. The idea of hybrid creatures permeates the world's cultures.

**Elongated Skulls:**[136] Elongated skulls have been found in Mexico,[137] close by the village of Onavas. Several truly alien-looking skulls were just recently unearthed from a cemetery. They are estimated to be around 1,000 years old.

Elongated skulls have also been found in Bolivia, Peru, and many other places around the globe.[138] In Asia, South America, as well as Europe, people buried those who had elongated skulls, some deliberately and abnormally elongated on purpose, apparently, or maybe not?

Supposedly, there were those humans who practiced binding their children's' heads[139] so that they would develop such elongated skulls. Why would they do this? If it was for a concept of beauty, where did such a concept that so grotesquely extended skulls were beautiful come from? Where did such an idea originate, and for what reason? More importantly, why was it so widespread, such a worldwide practice of so many?

Perhaps, these humans were just emulating their overlords of long ago? Were they attempting to paint themselves as the legitimate recipients of the gods' powers by imitating them, trying to outwardly, at least, resemble them? This would seem to be a distinct possibility.

Not only did they do this, but by the elongating of skulls as a global practice, this would seem to show that whoever they were emulating had global influence. It's said the sincerest form of flattery is imitation.

One other thing of note here: The practice of binding skulls to elongate them would seem to date back at least 9,000 years and quite probably more. This puts its origins at right around the time of Megalithia. Did the aliens, or at least some of them, have elongated skulls? Did we try to imitate this? It seems a distinct possibility at least one species of aliens did.

**Starchild:**[140] Found in Mexico, the Star Child skull is a truly unique object. It has been repeatedly investigated, and the results have been contradictory, to say the least. The child's skull is abnormally large for the size body it had. At first, this was thought to be a case of congenital hydrocephalus, a natural illness. Some researchers still claim that. Most now don't think that's the answer.

They point out that the skull does not have the standard deformed features of a hydrocephalus child. DNA testing said the child was completely human, according to at least one laboratory. Later testing in another laboratory said the child was only half-human, and the other half of the DNA was, quote, "unknown."

There is even a very involved group called The Starchild Project, which has investigated this matter at some length, and which firmly believes the child is only a half-human. They further say the makeup of the skull is fibrous, whereas with humans, skulls are not.[141] Therefore, the controversy still rages.

As researchers ourselves, normally we might be inclined to agree with the debunkers of the Starchild. After all, one skull does not prove an entire hybrid human race created by aliens, and partly in their image, ever existed. However, as always in this book, there is more. There is the matter of the Boskop people. Moreover, this is no hoax.

**Boskop People**: We've mentioned these people in another book and for good reason. They are like a people out of time, out of their proper place. As we just said above, if it was a case of just one skull being strange, we would dismiss the idea of hybrid humans out of hand. Nevertheless, the Boskop people are an intriguing discovery. When the first skull was discovered in 1913, it was quite an event. Right from the start controversy raged.

Numerous interpretations have been placed on the findings. Some said it was not even human at all, but some type of ape. Others brought up the same argument as with the Starchild skull, declaring it might have been hydrocephalus causing the unusually large dimensions of the skull, which was estimated to be a good 30% larger in cranial capacity than the average human skull of today.

However, the hydrocephalus theory now has been ruled out, since more skulls were later found and they, too, are of similar size and shape. Archaeologists and paleontologists decided the Boskop people were human after all, but just a variation hominid, a strange variation with a brain capacity well above our own.

As we have said, the controversy still rages. Debunkers are

rife. Oddly, in this case, so are the adherents. Some of them are quite prestigious. *New Scientist* magazine published a balanced article on the Boskop People. The *Discover* magazine did a positive article on the topic, as well, which immediately raised cries of "unfair and wrong" from the more determined skeptics. It seems no subject when it comes to the history of humanity and the idea of aliens is without such debate. Many times, such debates descend into the acrimonious.

One interesting side note here is that so much larger were the Boskop People's skulls compared to our own, that some reputable scientists say they may well have viewed the world through a completely different perspective than we did. In fact, they may have been so much more intelligent than we may be that they simply couldn't survive as a species in a time when life was so incredibly primitive.

They simply may not have been up to it. Something more brute-like, meaning us, would have the advantage over the Boskops, it seems, in a harsh and unforgiving world, one that was all claw, tooth, and nail in nature.

Were the Boskop People just too sensitive, able to view things from too many sides to be good decision makers in such a barbarous world? Were they just born out of their time? Were they an alien experiment that didn't work? Were they already what we may someday get to become? We'd give a lot to know the answers to those questions.

**Egypt Another Example:**[142] A pharaoh mentioned in passing earlier on, who went by the name of Akhenaten, is clearly depicted as having an elongated skull. Then there is the matter of the style of helmets many of the Egyptian pharaohs wore (and so favored?) These were clearly elongated in an odd shape, one that when placed on the head gave the pharaoh an appearance of having an elongated skull that bent slightly backwards. In addition, there are hieroglyphic depictions of other rulers with elongated heads, as well.

Ancient Egyptian legends refer to the first rulers of their kingdom as being a half, or mixed race. These beings were said to have been demigods, hybrids of the sky guardians and humans. They had elongated heads, as well, and these "demigods" were, according to Egyptian accounts of their earliest history, the first to rule Egypt. So very much a part of the Egyptian culture traces its origin as a kingdom and seems to revolve around the sky guardians with their elongated heads, that for millennia afterwards, pharaohs would wear elongated helmets to resemble them.[143]

Why did they? Some suggest that the helmet/crown of later pharaohs was styled after the sky guardians' heads deliberately, and not just because those with elongated skulls once had to wear them. This was to give later pharaohs the same look, and so supposedly imbued them with the same sense of semi-godhood as the sky guardians, the same divinity, as it were.

For countless generations, the Egyptians did think of their pharaohs as gods on earth, divine personages, and the true inheritors of the power from the sky gods themselves. When pharaohs died, they were thought to journey back to the heavens to join those gods. Therefore, the wearing of such crowns/helmets wasn't just out of tradition, but it was also to enhance the human rulers' power and rights of divinity, to rule, it seems.

**Peru is yet another example:**[144] As mentioned above, elongated skulls have been found in Peru, as well, and in abundance. Along the Paracas Peninsula, south of Lima, were discovered various stone implements. These came in different sizes and shapes. They were used for many purposes. A preliminary analysis of these items suggests they date back as far as 8,000 years ago. Found there, as well, was a graveyard where entire families were buried in tombs together. Moreover, they found elongated skulls, ones "enormously" elongated in some cases.[145]

**Russia and Iraq are yet more examples:**[146] In 2009, elongated skulls were found in Siberia. In Iraq, an elongated skull was found that might well be 45,000 years old! Now please remember, we're talking about people supposedly binding the heads of their children well back into the high period of the last Ice Age! What's more, apparently people around the world were engaged in this practice. Some researchers claim the elongations were done by binding a baby's head to wood boards, thus forcing the skull to grow in the elongated shape.

However, even they admit that this is only a theory. The idea they were doing this 45,000 years ago, some 37,000 years before our civilizations began, would seem a little hard to believe.

Wasn't it more likely these children might actually have been the hybrid offspring of humans and a species of aliens? It's either that, or we have fundamentally, and at the deepest level, gotten the entire history of civilization completely wrong!

**China and Europe Elongated Skulls:** Even China, too, has had its share of elongated skulls.[147] The same is true of Tibet, as well. All around the globe, it seems, and including Europe in such places as Norway and France, there were once people with elongated skulls. Whether they intentionally had had their heads bound to be this way, in emulation of some other species, or just naturally elongated skulls, is uncertain in many cases.

Therefore, the prevalence of elongated skulls on a global scale is not a question.[148] Just why this is so is a matter for conjecture, for it's a truly odd thing for such disparate cultures over such a vast amount of time to have in common.

Just why would people deliberately shape their children's skulls in such a strange fashion? And did they? The idea of binding a child's head, as feet were once bound, is just a theory, at best. But if they did do this why?

Were they trying to imitate their alien overlords? Did we, as a subjugated people, desire to look as much like our overlords, our masters, as possible? Maybe, it was in the belief that those who had similar shaped heads as the alien overlords would also possess their sorts of intelligence and power.

For more on the subject, we recommend a book titled, *The Enigma of Cranial Deformation* by David Hatcher Childress. His book goes much more into depth about the whole question of cranial deformation, and elongated skulls than we can here. He arrives at some very interesting and intriguing conclusions.

So are we an imitation of our alien rulers? In the Bible, in Genesis, it states that man was made in God's image. The Sumerian texts say much the same thing. So were we fashioned to resemble our alien overlords? More to the point, did we also, on a worldwide scale, often try to make ourselves look more like our overlords? Alternatively, were some of us hybrids and so resembled them more than others? We don't know for sure, but there might be a distinct possibility this was so.

However, were these, the only rulers of our world? Were there other aliens? If one goes by the Vedic texts of India, there were. Some appear to have been reptilian in nature. Others are described as being feathered and/or serpent like. The Hindu Vedas refer to there being over 400,000 species of humans and so-called subhumans. Aliens formed a substantial part of this group according to their texts.

If this were so, it would go a long way to explaining many myths about goblins, gnomes, elves, fairies, pixies, and such other so-called "fairy folk." What if they were really just different species of humans or aliens? Perhaps they were given such fanciful names, because they might have been shorter, taller, or with different features, appearing deformed and strange to us?

A case in point would be the so-called Human Hobbits of the island of Flores, who existed around 17,000 years ago.[149] Thought to be nonhuman, a different species of ape at first, they have since been categorized as human.

The "hobbits" were a very tiny people, only about three feet tall and weighing on average only 70 pounds. This made them a good deal smaller than the Pygmy People of today. Were these little people, or ones like them, the origin of the myth about elves?

One more point about the Vedic texts. They believed in other worlds, other planets from which many of these beings came, just as the Sumerian cuneiform texts believed the Anunnaki came from another world. The Vedic texts also said the aliens fought wars on Earth and in space. They even said one battle took place on the moon. Interesting, isn't it? How could Hindu texts somebody wrote thousands of years ago, know about other planets and space? Yet, they seem to have.[150]

As we mentioned earlier, in the New World, the Mayans believed their God was in the form of a feathered serpent. As this says:

> *"Kukulkan ("Plumed Serpent," "Feathered Serpent") is the name of a Maya snake deity that also serves to designate historical persons. The depiction of the feathered serpent deity is present in other cultures of Mesoamerica."*[151]

**—Wikipedia**

We find it interesting how the god, Kukulkan, spilled over into other religions of other civilizations in the area, as well. Was this so powerful a legend and tradition, had such force and strength among the peoples of the New World, that it would continue for so long? Did it spread, only taking slightly different forms throughout the entire region?

It seems it did. Little is known about the mythology of Kukulkan. The belief is mostly unexplained still. Why is this god such a powerful and enduring concept in the culture of the native peoples of the New World?

The Chinese have a long tradition of dragons having ruled the skies. Here, though, the reason might be a little different. Repeatedly in ancient Chinese literature, there are references made to flying dragons that spit fire, and gods coming out of the bellies of the things.

The first Emperor of China is referred to as the "Yellow Emperor." He was said to have emerged from a dragon. Was he of a different race than humans? Why would his own people give him such a designation?

Were the dragons actually spaceships or airborne vessels?

Remember they did have "gods" who would ride inside of them and disembark when they landed. These stories absolutely permeate Chinese legends, or as they refer to it, their history.[152] Therefore, whether one talks of dragons, serpents, or feathered serpents, the theme of such gods or demigods reoccurs often.

**Chapter Conclusion:** So all this just might give us a good idea of what the rulers of the Empire of Megalithia were like. If one is to believe any of our sources, any of the varied legends, myths, and histories of innumerable peoples around the planet at all, the many depictions we have of their gods, the numerous strange items discovered by archeologists, then one has to think certain things about the rulers of Megalithia must be true. Let's recap these here:

**1.** It would appear likely the supreme rulers of Megalithia were not human and not of this Earth, judging by all the legends and myths, as well as various depictions of these "gods" throughout history. We also have the Vedas and the Sumerian texts to refer to about this, as well.

**2.** Not only were they alien, but there could well have been more than one race of aliens involved. In fact, if we are to believe the Vedic and Sumerian writings, the various legends/histories of China, as well as those of the Mayans, not to mention ancient Egypt, and even the legends of North American native peoples, then these creatures came from our skies. We keep hearing this as a constantly recurring theme.

In addition, not only does there seem to be more than one type of alien, but with some seemingly closely resembling us, while others were far different. Or is it that we were made to resemble them, those with the elongated skulls, perhaps?

**3.** Our alien overlords were not a pleasant bunch of creatures. According to the Sumerian records of the Anunnaki, they liked to live in palaces, and liked to be waited on (served) by human slaves and servants. Thus, the human servants in the temple were the priests of the day. The priests of today still "serve God" in the temples we have now, only he is no longer physically there. Once, He, or some facsimile claiming to be Him, might have been.

**4.** Those priests were considered special. It would seem they were also accorded more privileges, as a result. More trust was placed in them, as with the human pilots of the Vimanas and others of that special class that closely served their Masters.

**5.** It would seem likely the aliens were few in number. If there had been great numbers of them, we should find more historical evidence for their having existed on Earth, unless somehow we just aren't recognizing it when we see such evidence, don't realize what it is we have. And there does seem to have been some tentative evidence that has been discovered. Even so, ten thousand years or more is a long time for any evidence to survive. Still, skeletons from burials, and such similar types of evidence should abound if Earth had a large population of aliens. We don't find this.

This could be for a number of reasons, including the fact they might have been cremated when they died. Even so, chance accidents with their vimanas or flying craft, should have allowed us to find some evidence for their existence in a physical sense. Again, although some evidence does seem to exist for just this sort of thing, and as we've shown here, controversy rages over the nature of it, and so we simply can't be sure.

Nevertheless, if they numbered in the millions or even billions, we would certainly have far more evidence of their existence today. We simply do not have this. What we really have are just tantalizing clues, tidbits of evidence that might or might not be significant. So again, it is our contention that the aliens were few in numbers.

**6.** They made up for this with their ability to quickly communicate and rapidly move about the planet. They traveled about in their flying machines to get from place to place on the earth. Since this privilege was restricted to only them and a few loyal humans, Megalithia was a place with a two-tiered transportation means.

For the rulers, it was flying. For humans, it was shanks pony. While our ancestors trudged across the Earth and so were limited to just a few miles, the aliens flew above us, circling the globe, and flitting from place to place whenever and wherever they liked.

Why do we reiterate this point? Because we feel their power over humanity should not be underestimated. Think of the tactical advantages flying would give the alien rulers. Think how the lack of any such transportation for us lesser beings would have kept us isolated, and quite probably deliberately so.

We've all heard of the old cliché "divide and conquer," but with the aliens, this was probably truer than with anyone else in our history. Isolated pockets of humanity in very small numbers, pose far less of a threat than a united population of greater numbers. This is just simple, good, political, and military strategy. That is, if one wants to maintain control of unwilling subjects.

**7.** Superior alien technology was the main means of keeping humanity under control. We just discussed this when it comes to their flying abilities, but it goes much farther than that. Based on the Sumerian texts of the Anunnaki, and the Vedic texts of India, as well as various other oral histories from around the world, it would appear our alien masters had much more than just capabilities of flying. We will get into that later on, as well, when we discuss their technology in depth.

For now, suffice it to say, the aliens were probably very good at controlling us, dominating us, and punishing us, if we stepped out of line. They had the means. They had the advantage of speed over us. They had the technological power.

By all accounts, their retribution was brutal and often. The aliens did not spare the rod to spoil the child, it seems, not if that child was human. We were not even considered a true species to them, but simply a subspecies of slaves, perhaps ones even created by them for just such a purpose, as the Sumerian texts say. They did grant some favors. However, this was just another form of manipulation, and it was reserved only for those who served them personally and well.

**8.** The aliens used puppet human rulers to help increase their control over humanity, and keep the aliens, personally, at a distance from us. Again, based on the records of the Anunnaki, it would seem the aliens rarely interacted with humans outside of their temples.

Perhaps they were too few in numbers safely to do this, were too vulnerable. Not being natives of Earth this could well have been the case. Even the air, filled with our germs, viruses, and fungal spores might have presented deadly consequences for them if they breathed it unfiltered. Whatever the reason, they seemed to prefer to stay distanced from humanity.

Why this emphasis of theirs on distancing themselves from humanity? Was it to increase the fear of them, as literally alien and unknown creatures? Or did they fear us? Perhaps both of these things that were the problem? Maybe, they simply found us physically revolting? Possibly, they just had a complete disdain for us, and didn't want us in their sight more than necessary?

Alternatively, it could be they preferred their human puppet rulers to take the brunt of humanity's anger. Let the masses, such as they were at the time, rise up against their human rulers when enraged, rather than attack the real powers behind the human thrones, the so-called "gods" in their "holy of holies," or temples.

It has been said that "distance lends enchantment" and it seems our alien rulers recognized this fact. By keeping "above it all," they could continue to be revered as virtual gods, instead of just alien creatures to be rebelled against. The excesses of their subordinate human rulers who carried out vile acts on their behalf wouldn't taint them. This is another impressive tactic on their part, if this is true. Human government could have been their scapegoat.

**9.** The aliens were long-term rulers. There are several reasons why we believe this is so. First, the very nature of the Megalithian Empire itself would seem to have been a hideously stable one. If there were rebellions, they almost certainly were all crushed, at least until the end came. As mentioned earlier and contrary to the themes of some popular television shows, movies, and novels, there have been no successful rebellions by slaves overcoming their rulers, at least, not without help from someone else.

Yes, we think of the American Revolution and the French Revolution as having been successful examples of people rising up against tyranny and winning the day. Nevertheless, if you look closer at these revolutions, you'll find the people involved, the lower classes, either had help from the middle and upper classes, or from outside.

While the American Revolution was going on, as we've said, England was, basically, in a world war, if you remember. She was battling the Dutch as well as the French and oftentimes the Spanish, not to mention the rebellious American colonies, and her opponents' colonies, as well. In addition, the French actively aided and abetted the new "Americans" with ships, soldiers, officers, and supplies.

The same is true of the French rebellion. The upper classes, for whatever their reasons, were actively involved in the revolution against the monarchy, as well. The actual rebellion may have started among the lower classes, but without the aid and support of the side-switching royal troops, and some of the nobility, it never would've won the day.

Even Spartacus, that so-famous slave rebel of ancient Rome, didn't win in the end. He ended up crucified along with a couple of thousands of other rebellious slaves for his troubles. There was never a long-term successful rebellion by slaves against their masters in Rome, Sparta, or any other civilization.

In South Africa, in recent times, Apartheid was only ended when those in power finally decided it should be, because world pressure to do so had been long and draining upon their resources. Economic boycotts had finally done their work.

This is by no means to lessen the efforts of brave people. However, no matter how brave a people are, it's hard to win a rebellion when the enemy has artillery, tanks, and jets, and you only have clubs, bows and arrows, and spears. Without outside aid of some sort, such rebellions invariably go down to defeat, however noble they may be, however right the cause. That's just reality.

So it is our contention the alien rulers of Megalithia, despite having to deal with rebellions on occasion, managed to maintain control of their Empire for a very long time. It may even have been tens of thousands of years.

Could this be why they built to last with their megalithic structures? Instead of things having to last decades, they very well might have needed to last hundreds of years, or even thousands. Hence, they may have had a need for building huge stone platforms and structures, so they could act as their spaceports and other necessities for long periods, a time so long that the structures would have to resist even the effects of natural erosion, let alone normal wear and tear on a daily basis.

**10.** We don't know the lifespan of the aliens, especially since it seems there was more than one species of them. However, with such a high level of technology where they can span the distance between stars, one would assume they had managed to increase their lifespans considerably with technological and medical means that do not exist yet on Earth.

Our lifespans are lengthening, even as we achieve greater technological and medical sophistication. One could safely assume the same would have held true for the aliens. In addition, there are the references to those who were hybrids of humans and the aliens as having extended lives, as well.

**11.** The aliens, at least some types of them, may have interacted with humans on a more intimate level, such as sexually. All around the world, legends and mythologies abound with the gods mating with human beings, especially women. Whether one looks at Greek legends, Mayan legends, northern European legends, or even Sumerian cuneiform texts, not to mention the native North American legends concerning star people, all talk about this interaction.

Is this even possible, for members of different species to

interact sexually? Well, it would be if we were created in their image, and resembled them physically in most ways. If we had similar DNA. Yes, this is a matter largely for conjecture, but even so it well may have happened. We feel there is enough anecdotal evidence to support the idea. Again, what are one person's myths is another person's history.

We in the West need to get over our chauvinistic attitude about the oral histories and the written ones of other people that don't seem to jibe with our own. Not to do this implies a strong arrogance on our part. In the process of learning to do this, we might just actually learn a few things. After all, the age of empires, colonialism, and imperialism are supposed to be over. We need to adjust our attitudes accordingly.

**12.** Were there any kind of compassionate aliens as our rulers? Yes, probably there were. Nothing is monolithic, and probably not even the nature of aliens, any more than it is for us. Although we say the alien masters were brutal, and lacking in compassion, this probably wasn't true in every single case. There are also many legends and myths worldwide that speak of the gods being kind to us. Prometheus, for example, gave the gift of fire to humanity. Was there an alien who once did this for humanity? Perhaps different species behaved differently to us. This doesn't seem to have happened nearly as often as the gods tricking and being cruel to us, though, just using us for their pleasure, but it does seem to have happened on occasion, possibly.

Now why did some of the so-called gods do this? We simply don't know. Perhaps, they had gone "native." Maybe, they had some personal ax to grind with their counterparts and giving us certain gifts acted to undermine those others.

This isn't such a strange idea. In America, opposing forces would arm the Native American Indians with rifles to cause problems for other colonials, as with the French versus the English. So maybe the gifts to us were just to cause trouble for other aliens.

Yes, that does seem to be a rather jaundiced way of looking at it, but when you read Sumerian texts about the Anunnaki, as translated, one doesn't get a very good impression of our alien gods. The same holds true for the Vedic texts.

**13.** Earth existed for the good of the mother planet. Again, it would appear the aliens practiced a very strong form of mercantilism, and/or colonialism. It seems either everything was directly for their benefit, or their peoples' benefit. Very little, if anything, was left over for humans. Our population was small.

Numerous books talk about the idea that genetic experiments were carried out upon us. Various authors have even suggested plagues and diseases were ways of controlling our population and helping to manifest those genetic changes, the not so natural selection of our genetic pool, to proceed the way they wished it to proceed. *Gods of Eden*,[153] by William Bramley, is one very good example of such work. It is comprehensive, in-depth, and a compelling look at the idea we were being periodically savaged with plagues and other diseases by aliens. Many other authors expound upon this subject, as well.

**14.** This is our last main point about how the aliens ruled over Megalithia. It would seem that not only was there more than one race, but perhaps many of them and most importantly of all, they didn't get along. The Anunnaki text describes constant conflicts among those rulers. Almost every culture on earth has myths and legends of the gods fighting with each other.

Oddly, all these myths and legends assigned different powers to different gods. Isn't that an interesting concept, and such a universal one? Perhaps the legends that come down to us today are really assigning one particular type of power to each kind of alien species. In other words, one god in a Hopi legend may actually represent an entire species.

One final thought about this last point. We think this is what finally brought about the downfall of Megalithia. Although the effects of this collapse for the aliens were catastrophic, for us humans it may have also spelled the end of the alien empire in this section of interstellar space. Again, we will discuss this more in depth in the next chapters.

Suffice it to say for now that something brought about the end of the alien Empire of Megalithia. Since it probably didn't come from within, a successful rebellion by us (at least not without outside help), then it must have arisen from factional warfare between the different alien species themselves.

Do we have evidence for this contention? Yes, we think we do, and plenty of it. What's more, we think it is highly detailed evidence.

# Chapter 12

## Strange Technologies of Megalithia

**M**egalithia may have differed from other empires that subsequently followed it in one remarkable way, and that's besides having aliens for its rulers. This has to do with its technology. Yes, one would assume that an alien race that could make it to Earth from some distant planet in another solar system must have a technology greater than our own. However, Megalithia's technology is so strange, it borders on being considered magic.

Ancient humans actually thought it was magic. We do not. But if the reports of what they could do are even half true, then they had control of forces that we do not, and even may have known of forces we don't yet know exist.

Why do we say this? Well, it has to do with a number of factors. Yes, some of their technology does seem to be an extrapolation of things even we can do now, but other aspects of their scientific abilities seem to be way beyond ours. If not exactly magic, they come darn close to it. Even so, as the famous author, Arthur C. Clarke, said, "Magic's just science that we don't understand yet."

Therefore, we define the technology of the Megalithian Empire as being in two basic categories. In the first, are those capabilities that we may not yet have ourselves, but which we can reasonably extrapolate as someday having, because we have an idea of what they might be, and have something, albeit much more basic, already along those lines.

For instance, we do not have a drive capable of getting us to another star system, at least not within any sort of a reasonable timeframe. To get to even the nearest star would take us hundreds, more likely thousands of years with today's technology. The alien rulers of Megalithia had some way of achieving this goal much faster. However, we recently came up with an Ion drive. Scientists are also considering using an atomic drive, one that literally uses tiny atomic explosions to accelerate a ship to incredible speeds in relatively short times. This would make a trip to Mars instead of being close to a year or more, just a matter of a few weeks. Still, even this system would not get us to the nearest star in a reasonable time. Nor could we probably carry the fuel necessary to get us there, in any case.

Whether or not the aliens had faster-than-light capabilities is unknown. At the minimum however, they must've had some type of ship drive that could bring them at least close to the speed of light. Either this or they had some other alternate means of traveling through space, such as via wormhole, some sort of warping drive, etc.

Yet, it is distinctly within the realm of possibility that we might come up with such a drive sometime in the next century or two. Scientists are already working from several different directions to achieve this goal, such as the Alcubierre Drive. Promulgated by the theoretical physicist, Miguel Alcubierre, a craft could travel the equivalent of faster-than-light using such a drive. It would do this by having the ship contract space in front of it and expand space behind it.[154] Therefore, the idea and even the possibility of faster-than-light travel, is not unknown to us. We are exploring the means themselves as to how to go about doing this.

If the drive they used involved some sort of energy we do not yet know exists, then that, of course, would put the technology into the other category of being completely unknown to us.

With regard to that second category, is the question of how the aliens might have lifted 1,000-ton stones? This, we have no idea, but only rudimentary guesses. The same holds true for ley lines. That they seem to exist is a fact. What they mean, or what they are, is still completely unknown to us. Again, we only have conjectures, some of them, perhaps, quite wild, but no real answers at all with regard to ley lines.

With the aliens' ability to fly about the planet, we have that now, so that technology is known to us, or at least something comparable to what they had is known. We may not use the same method they did, but we have analogous techniques, ones that achieve pretty much the same results and in the same timeframe.

What of the unknown technologies they possessed? What were they like? Let's look at some evidence we've come across for some of the possible capabilities of those ancient rulers of Megalithia. These items come from various sources, but we have provided links for those who wish to explore them further. As with all our endnotes throughout this document, one can link directly to the actual sites from which we obtained the information.

So let's start with something discovered rather recently. That is, did the ancient aliens have a defensive shield around Earth to stop other alien intruders at one time? Here's an interesting news item from Russia that might just shed some light on that subject:

**Alien Defense Shield:**[155] According to a report, researchers traveled to Siberia to investigate rumors and reports of items of technology that were apparently alien and ancient in origin. There had been reported numerous sightings over time and long-term rumors of some sort of objects of strange technology, the exact nature of which, remained elusive, but which were described as large "cauldrons."

The researchers claim they did find something and they have photographs to prove it.[156] Bizarre articles, they were made of metal. Five of them, were found in a swampy region. These objects were sunken in the boggy water there, but according to local people, who had periodically reported on these things, at one time the metal devices had been above water, had been "high and dry." The location of the discoveries is precisely where old legends said they were.

~ **149** ~

Myths tell of these objects forming part of a defense shield of our planet. Incoming objects from space with a potential to threaten Earth would cause these cauldron-like devices to trigger, shoot up fireballs, and somehow deflect or destroy whatever was approaching from space, even meteors. Was this to stop their enemies from using small asteroids as kinetic weapons? It's possible.

Several of the scientists included on the research team even openly speculated if this supposed defensive shield might have even triggered the infamous Tunguska blast, which was, according to researchers, an aerial burst over the same general region in 1908.[157] They further noted that this area has been known for several large meteor strikes in the past. Apparently, statistically, there have been an unusually high number of these. Are these objects being "shot" down by this defensive shield, is there question.

Made of a "copper-like metal," that seems to be an extremely hard alloy resistant to damage, such as scratches, these "cauldrons" or "domes" (depending on whether they are still right side up or not), are spread over a wide region. The outer edges of the things had "sharp points" on them.[158]

The initial research group included one astrophysicist, three geologists, one mechanical engineer and three research assistants. Two of this group became ill while investigating there.

There is strong evidence of people who visit the area coming down with radiation sickness. Detractors of this state that, yes, people have sickened from radiation in the region, but this was because it was home to the old Soviet Union's testing area for nuclear weapons.

Proponents of the UFO/defensive shield theory contradict this argument and point out that a history of such "sicknesses" date back long before any nuclear tests took place there, several centuries, at least. They further point out that the area's name in the local dialect is ""Uliuiu Cherkechekh," which translates means, "The Valley of Death."

This is not a new appellation, but dates far back, long before the old Soviet Union existed, and according to them, the name is deserved. In addition, they claim "forest demons" are responsible for having placed them there and that the objects cause people and animals in the area to sicken and die.

Others argue that the circular holes in the swamp (filled with water now) are the result of an ancient UFO battle in the skies overhead, and some of those craft subsequently crashed there.

Now, when we say reports and myths go far back about these "cauldrons," they do! They go so far back that geographical features have long been named for them.

As an example, in Suntar there is the Algy Timirbit stream. This translates from the local native dialect to "the large cauldron sank. Near there is said to be a large cauldron, partly buried but with full-grown trees growing inside of it. Supposedly, it is from this cauldron the stream originally derived its names, just as the "Valley of Death," seems connected to people over the centuries dying of a strange "sickness." The cauldrons all seem to be quite large; being at least over 18 feet in diameter and with edges so sharp, they can "cut a fingernail."

In a passage from a letter penned in 1996 by another person who visited the Valley of Death, Mikhail Koretsky from Vladivostok wrote that he felt there were a lot of them in the area. He and friends even spent a night sleeping in one of the cauldrons and that the things were about six to nine meters in diameter.

He furthers states in his letter they seemed to be made of "some strange metal," that resembled copper but which he felt sure actually wasn't, because it was simply too hard. Mikhail said that even their hammers barely made a dent in the material. He and his comrades attempted to break a piece off a cauldron, but found the metal was simply too hard to do so and seemed to be covered with a material that resembled "emery," but wasn't.

After sleeping in the cauldron, Mikhail and his friend noticed no ill effects. However, about three months later, one of them lost their hair and Mikhail developed "three small sore spots" on his head that never went away. These appeared on the side of his face he had slept on in the cauldron.

According to another researcher, N. D. Arkhipov, he refers to the existences of "bronze" cauldrons near the upper area of the river there. In the native tongue, "olguis," means cauldron. The name of the river there is—you guessed it—Olguidakh, or "Cauldron Stream." The area is rife with ancient legends of the cauldrons, and has been for a very long time.

So is it possible our ancient aliens of Megalithia had installed a planetary shield, perhaps against asteroids or meteors being used as kinetic weapons? Perhaps, they did. By the way, this report comes from numerous different sources, not just Pravda.

**Puma Punku—Again:** We are bringing up the subject of Puma Punku again to mention several additional things about this site that fall under this topic, rather than the previous one. First, the name, "Puma Punku" means, "Puma Gate." Of course, this immediately begs the question—the gate to what?

Secondly, many claim the scattered "machined" H-blocks found there, date back 12,000 to 15,000 years ago. At an average weight of about 100 tons, these blocks aren't light! They come from a quarry some 15 kilometers from the actual site.[159] Some are as much as 400 tons in weight. Metal clamps were used to keep the larger blocks together. Again, this places Puma Punku right smack in the middle of the Age of Megalithia, and some 2,000 years, at least, or more, before humans were supposed to have even been using metal in such a way.

Depictions of men with beards seem to illustrate that whoever built this site were not the indigenous people, who do not grow beards well, if at all. In addition, when we say the stones were cut with precision, we mean precision! There are only millimeters or less in the variance of each of them. This would be hard to accomplish even now. The holes in the blocks we mentioned earlier in the prior section are all cut precisely to the same depth and with the same diameters.

Now, as interesting as this is, why do we mention Puma Punku again? Well, because of the similarities to such sites in Europe and Asia. First, the bearded men depicted are strangely reminiscent of the depiction of the Anunnaki. Secondly, the stones seem to have the same history as those of the platforms in Baalbek and the Dome of the Rock. That is, nobody knows how they were moved to those locations. Thirdly, the indigenous people near Puma Punku claim that some sort of magic was used to float the stones, just as "magic" was used by the Anunnaki. "Demons," "djinn," or giants were supposedly involved in those other places, as well. As we also mentioned earlier, even the Great Pyramids of Giza have legends by the ancient Egyptians of blocks of stone being made somehow to float.

This is why we bring up Puma Punku again, because we have worldwide references to some sort of "magic" being used. This "magic" to float colossal stones about, sounds a lot like antigravity of some sort, or something similar, some unknown energy being used. Concerning creating and moving about massive blocks of stone, they all have one thing in common—their size and the precision with which they were made. Finally, they all seem to date back to the same period, that is, the time of the Megalithian Empire.

So we have global stories of creation and moving of massive stones, and the accompany legends of beings, "sky people," etc., using "magic" to move them about. This means we have the hard evidence of the stones themselves (pun intended), and the softer, but still prevalent evidence of the verbal histories of peoples around the world, as well as the cuneiform written records of the Sumerians, Egyptian hieroglyphics, and such. This constitutes a fair amount of evidence, all told.

**Peruvian Stargate:**[160] In southern Peru in the mountainous area of Hayu Marca, there is something referred to constantly as a stargate. One of the interesting things one first becomes aware of in this particular instance is that the so-called "stargate" is just about 22 miles from Puno, a city that has long been noted as being the "city of the gods."

Again, we have those local geographical names for things related to something from "out there." This gives us an indication of just how long such stories persist, that areas and regions end up named for them, as with the cauldrons in Siberia, or the "star" towns and villages along a ley line in Europe.

The Stargate itself is carved into the side of a rocky outcrop. The gate is roughly rectangular, and stands about 23 feet high and 23 feet wide. In the center of the carved depression that forms the "doorway," is another smaller depression, oddly shaped. This was said to be a place where one, usually a high priest, inserted a "key" of some sort.

This allowed one to pass through the rock wall by transforming it into a doorway into another realm, the realm of the gods, hence the name, Puerta de Hayu Marca, which in English translates to "gate of the gods."

Also of note is the fact that Westerners only discovered this gate in 1996. Of course, the native people of the area had long known about it. However, they never spoke of it. The Stargate was considered one of the best-kept secrets, but then one has to wonder why.

Why keep it such a secret? As with so many such sites, there are old local legends concerning the stargate. Again, the stargate was known as a gateway to the gods' realm. If one could pass through it, one can join them and be immortal. Sometimes, priests would return with some of the gods. Moreover, these visitations had all the hallmarks of being inspection tours. After inspecting the earthly realm, they would then swiftly return through the gate.

Another local legend says that when the Spanish conquistadors invaded Peru and began to steal anything that was precious in the way of gold and jewels, an Incan priest, Aramu Maru,[161] fled before them, carrying a golden disk, which was considered most sacred. This disc was known as the "key of the gods of the seven rays."

Later, after hiding in the mountains near the Stargate, and

after completing a sacred right, with the shaman already there, he placed the key in the depression. A tunnel opened. Blue light bathed them all. They then handed the key to the shamans, and passed on through the gate. He was never to return.

Now this is interesting. The story is very specific. It refers to (1) a key that fits in the depression. Yes, the depression is carved into the rock, as if meant to have something placed within it. (2) The priest does not pass through with the key, but gives it to the shamans before he goes. Presumably, this would mean the key is still in our realm, here on Earth. (3) The description of his passing through the gate is also interesting.

Apparently, a tunnel appears, blue light shines forth from it. Aramu Maru enters the tunnel and it closes behind him. He is never seen again. Yet, on occasion, sometimes these travelers did come back, hand-in-hand with the gods, Finally, (4) the nearby city of Puno has long been known as the "city of the gods," which is curious in itself, and makes it seem related to the Stargate.

If one puts all this together, we have a sacred area of the gods, a priesthood apparently devoted to them, a doorway known as a Stargate that allows people and aliens to pass back and forth through it. At one time, Western researchers would have put this down as being pure myth, legends of magic.

Now, with the idea that wormholes may well exist, this story doesn't seem quite so farfetched, does it? A wormhole would literally be a tunnel to somewhere "else." Some scientists say that "somewhere else" may not even be in our universe. Also interesting to note is the fact that wormholes are considered tunnels, for one could conceivably pass through it either way.

One other intriguing aspect of this legend is the last part of it says that one day the gate will open. When it does, it will be much larger, and allow the gods to pass through to us in their "sun ships." Are we talking an alien invasion here?

As another side note, we would mention that the Stargate there is a close resemblance to the Gate of the Sun at Tiahuanaco. Nor are these the only antique sites. There are at least five other such sites. If one draws a grid pattern, they center near Lake Titicaca, on the plateau there. We would also mention that numerous UFO sightings constantly are seen in this area. What that means, exactly, we're not sure, but again, it's an intriguing thing to note.

Why did we mention the Stargate here? What does it have to do with ancient aliens? Well, for one thing, the site is old, really old. In addition, it has one of the hallmarks of Megalithia, in that it is carved out of stone. Once again, other features of the region seem to relate by their names to it, as with "city of the gods."

There is one more reason why we included the Peruvian Stargate here. The Sumerians, too, have a depiction of the so-called "Sumerian Stargate." This image shows a figure standing in the doorway. So again, we have these odd connections around the planet with regard to structures of stone, ancient names, as well as legends and superstitions abounding about them, and always that connection with the Sumerian, and their infamous Anunnaki.[162]

If this constantly seems to be the case with regard to these sorts of things, the Stargates, etc., reoccurring in different areas the world, then it would seem incumbent upon us, to at some point, realize there is a connection. This is not just a tenuous one, either, not just another coincidence that keeps repeating itself so specifically and unvaryingly, and all around the planet.

Nor does anyone say that the Peruvian Stargate is a hoax. People argue over its real purpose, whether it truly was a Stargate or not, but they don't argue the fact that it exists, that it's old, and that somebody carved it for some reason or other, and that reason is currently unknown.

One such "Stargate" may be an anomaly. Two such Stargates may be an odd coincidence. When there are more, then you really do have to ask yourself why they exist at all, and why they are a recurring theme in such widely separate places on Earth.

**Pyramids of Giza as a power plant:**[163] We've already discussed how the age of the Pyramids may be far older than the time set by mainstream Egyptologists. We've also mentioned there are strange oddities about the pyramids, that one seems to have even suffered an ancient internal explosion and part of it had been reconstructed.

However, here we wanted to focus on the idea that the pyramids might have been power plants of some sort. We'll keep this short, but we did want to mention, only in passing at least, that some are arguing the pyramid was a way of creating hydrogen, that the shafts we mentioned earlier on were to facilitate this process. Christopher Dunn wrote a well-received book on the subject.[164]

The resulting hydrogen was then burned to run some sort of generating equipment that might have allowed a beam of microwave energy to go into space. This microwave beam could have acted as a source of power for vehicles in orbit around the Earth. It is theorized it might have been used to power spaceships or satellites of some sort. Alternatively, perhaps the energy was used in that "defensive shield."

Since the mid-Twentieth Century, people have argued the shape of the pyramid itself has unusual properties and could act as a conduit for some type of mysterious energy flowing from the Earth, itself that they acted to focus such energy. With the discovery there are far more pyramids than were ever thought to exist, ones buried on land, as well as having sunk below the sea,[165] we have to wonder just why so many were built.

Either the ancients had a real penchant for building pyramids for no apparent reason, other than as incredibly elaborate and expensive tombs (when there is really no sign inside of them of this being the purpose as there is with all real Egyptian tombs), or they had to have some other reason for having them built. Again, the idea of energy keeps bubbling up and a mysterious energy at that, one unknown to us today. Now with the discovery of Dark Energy, perhaps this isn't such a far-out idea as people might once have thought.

**Ark of the Covenant as an alien device:**[166] According to

Paul Schroeder, "there is overwhelming evidence that the Ark of the Covenant was structurally designed to act as both an alien transmitter-capacitor and weapon."[167]

He points out that according to the Bible and many stories about the Ark, if one touched it unprotected, one would die. As with many other scholars with regard to the Ark of the Covenant, who say that there seems to be evidence it was a communication device, Paul Schroeder feels the same way. He gives very interesting arguments, backed by many facts, to bolster his position.

It is his contention and others that the Ark was a means of communicating with aliens and not God. He, again along with others, contends the Ark was also used to intervene in battles and decisively on the side of the Israelites. Somehow, this very strange piece of technology appears to have been siding with the Chosen People. It would appear whoever these strangers were, they had an intimate and vested interest in the outcome of what happened to the Israelites.

Again, many other researchers feel the same way. They point out the following quotations from the Bible:

> *"And they shall make an Ark of shittim wood, two cubits and a half shall be the length thereof, and a cubit and a half the breadth thereof, and a cubit and a half the height thereof.*
>
> *"And thou shalt overlay it with pure gold, within and without shalt thou overlay it, and shalt make upon it a crown of gold around and all about."*

**—Exodus 25:10**

There's that use of gold again. Of course, this isn't all of it. Those who were to be intimate with the Ark had to wear special clothing, and even special sandals. Those who were not properly dressed, wearing the correct sandals, would die. The Ark was also supposed to have an oracle, a place from which a voice issued forth, supposedly that of God.

In addition, the Bible mentions people did die just by merely touching the Ark. A friend of David, a man by the name of Uzzah, died touching the Ark. As the Bible says:

> *"Uzzah put forth his hand to the Ark of God, and took hold of it, for the oxen shook it. And the anger of the Lord was kindled against Uzzah, and God smote him there for his error, and there he died by the Ark of God."*

**—2 Samuel 6:6**

He wasn't the only one. During one of the battles, the Philistines managed to take the Ark. This had disastrous consequences for them. Fifty thousand Philistines died as a result, dropping on the spot. Thereupon, they promptly sent the Ark back to the Hebrews. Who wouldn't under such circumstances?

Now, we don't want to belabor this topic too much, because so many have spoken on it before already. Suffice it to say, it would appear unlikely that God would require people to build an Ark in a certain way, using a certain type of wood for poles to carry it, and forcing people to wear certain types of clothing and sandals for protection while doing this.

An omnipotent God, that is an all-powerful God, simply wouldn't require his followers to use such elaborate means to protect themselves. An all-powerful God could do that for them, without telling them to resort to wearing special sandals, special clothing, and making everything out of a special wood, which by the way, was highly nonconductive, even for wood.

What's more, the consequences of not following these orders to the letter resulted in rather hideous deaths. The descriptions of those dying from having contact with the Ark include what seem to be symptoms of receiving fatal amounts of radiation, probably electrical in nature. The Ark was most likely a piece of alien technology.

Since the Ark was deliberately designed and given to the Israelites by someone they thought of as God, with provisions that it be used to help win battles, and as a means for God to communicate directly with Moses, we can only assume someone wanted close-up control of this particular native people of Earth.

We can also assume the Ark had powers and included among these was acoustical power, since it could generate the voice of "God" for Moses to listen to, and he could respond in kind. Moreover, the aliens didn't seem to mind killing friends or foes, if they didn't follow their orders exactly. Failure to do so, to handle the Ark as directed, resulted in the penalty of rather hideous deaths. "God," it seems, wasn't particularly lenient in this regard.

Consequently, it would appear that any means justified their ends. This seems to be in direct keeping with the behavior of those aliens in control of Megalithia. We have no reason to believe it wasn't the same ones.

**Strange Sound or Acoustic Weapons:**[168] The walls of Jericho, now there is a strange story from the bible! The Israelites had marched into the Promised Land. They were told they must conquer Jericho. Whereupon, they marched around the outer walls of the city for days and lugging the Ark of the Covenant along with them each time. On the seventh such circuit, when completed, they blew their trumpets, and the walls of Jericho "come-a tumblin' down," as one famous old song put it.

This tale is interesting because the need to follow a certain and very specific set of instructions to the letter seems fundamental in the telling of it. God did not simply wave his hand and collapse the walls of Jericho. Instead, the Israelites were forced to go through an elaborate, lengthy, and time-consuming process to achieve their goal. What's more, it specifically involves using the Ark of the Covenant each time.

Something strange certainly seems involved here. This time, according to the Hebrew Testament, there was a need of both the

Ark and the horns in order to accomplish the job. Therefore, we know the Ark had special acoustic capabilities, as well as communication ones. Were these acoustic capabilities involved along with the horns in destroying the outer walls of Jericho? Was it an amplifier? Did it amplify sound, cause a destructive sympathetic vibration to destroy the walls, even as sympathetic vibrations can destroy bridges?

Then there is the god, Thor of Norse mythology, who used a hammer to smite his foes to the accompaniment of explosive sounds. Moreover, the voice of God was supposed to kill anyone who heard it, unless somehow protected by Him.

If the idea of the aliens having such things as acoustic weapons seems ridiculous, think again. We have and are still developing them right now. They are of particular interest to the military and law enforcement. One of the reasons for this is that they, in some cases, are non-lethal. As far back as the 1970s, it is believed that a prototype ultrasonic riot control was used during some riots.

One such piece of equipment, the "squawk box," was able to send out two different and "intolerably high-pitched ultrasonic frequencies" at rioters.[169] This caused such an uncomfortable sensation for the rioters that they no longer wanted to be within range of the device.

Oddly, neither the military nor law enforcement agencies have ever admitted using the device. They don't even admit to its existence. Yet, at Information Unlimited, elaborate instructions are available for building a Phasor Pain Field Generator. Not only this, but there are plans available there, ones enabling people to build handheld versions, as well. So the idea ancient aliens couldn't have had such incredible weapons is just wrong. That aliens may have used such devices isn't really so farfetched at all, not if we have them now.

**Deadly Beam Weapons:** There seems to be much historical evidence in the form of legends, myths, and even historical records from the Vedic texts, as well as the Sumerian cuneiform tablets, and from around the globe in general, for the gods (think ancient aliens here) using some type of beam weaponry.

The Greek god, Zeus, threw lightning bolts. Odin is said to have had some type of "spear" which when used, would send forth lightning bolts. In the Vedic texts of the Mahabharata, the aliens were supposed to have had some type of beam weaponry. This involved a reflector to focus the light, no less. This was a killing or death ray, supposedly. The God of the Old Testament was called upon to hurl lightning bolts. In Psalm 144:6, it says:

*Send forth lightning and scatter the enemy;*

Moreover, in written records from ancient historical times, we have the use of beams as weapons by unknown agents repeatedly mentioned. Alexander the Great, for instance, apparently had the help of alien UFOs when he was attacking the city of Tyre.[170]

Now strangely, two biblical prophets had prophesized the fall of Tyre well before it had occurred, before Alexander ever came on the picture. Nevertheless, it is the description of how it fell that fascinates and so pertains to this topic of beam weaponry.

The chief historian for Alexander wrote that during the assault on the city "gleaming silver shields" (again, we have those shields showing up) in the sky used a 'beam of light' which resulted in a section of the wall of the fortified city to collapse. It sounds rather like the walls of Jericho, doesn't it? However, this was with an exception. Here, it was a light beam and not sound that seems to have done the job.

Strangely, it wasn't just Alexander's historian claiming this occurred. Tyre's historians, as well, say the same thing. They give the exact same reason for the fall of their city. This is a strong form of corroboration, because when the losers of a battle agree with the victors on how it was lost, one would think this was unlikely, unless it was true.

An odd thing about Alexander the Great; he seems to have

been plagued by those "flying silver shields" throughout his campaigns. As mentioned, they were even said to have stopped his attack in India by buzzing his troops and "maddening" his elephants. Ultimately, so demoralized were his troops by this event that he was forced to turn around from his invasion of India and head back west.

Again, it sounds like we have an extraterrestrial agency controlling events on Earth, the very outcomes of them by direct and open meddling. When necessary, they were sometimes quite out in the open about this, blatantly so. How can we account for this when the aliens supposedly disappeared along with Megalithia? Well, in our final chapter, we will attempt to explain this.

However, our point here is that if this sort of thing has happened in recorded history, and by more than one party of witnesses to it, then it is hardly inconceivable to think it might've happened earlier in our history, during the age of Megalithia. The Vedas seem to support this contention. They declare the aliens had such weaponry.

**Ancient Depictions of Flying Objects:**[171] When we talk of Megalithia, we keep trying to provide evidence for the existence of it and its ruling class, the aliens. Since one of our main contentions is that aliens ruled Megalithia and had flying machines, whether spaceships and/or craft that flew through the air around the globe, it would seem we're stretching.

However, we're not. All through the history of humanity these sorts of things have been observed, reported, as well as had pictures drawn of them, and even been included in paintings. They have been written about extensively.

The Bible seems to have many examples of this last. We won't go into detail about those, but very few of us have not seen on television, or read about prophets being taken up in flying craft, or descending in them. One prophet was even given instructions on how to build a landing stadium for such a vehicle and in detail.

Nevertheless, since our space is limited here, we thought we would concentrate on examples that are more recent. The reason we wish to do this is to show that there is ample evidence even from just centuries ago, of flying objects in our skies. If they were flying then, it isn't such a leap, is it, to think they might've been flying even longer ago, as well? Let's cite just a few examples here:

**The Madonna with Saint Giovannino:**[172] A 15th century painting and we see Mary in the foreground, but the background you should pay particular attention to. There is a spiky looking UFO hovering in the sky there. Moreover, lest you think it was some sort of anomaly, notice the man standing on the hillside looking up at it, with his arm raised to shield his eyes from the glare so that he can better view the object.

What would fly in the sky at that time that an artist would or could paint? Yes, he might paint birds, but not much else floated around the sky at the time and especially not in broad daylight in the 1400s. Certainly, there were no balloons, airplanes, or any sort of fabricated aircraft. In addition, this object certainly doesn't look natural. It is quite artificial in appearance and distinctly metallic in nature.

One thing that should be remembered here is that artists of the time, when they saw or heard about such strange things in the skies, took them to be signs or portents of God. Therefore, it was usual for them to include them in their religious pictures.

**The Baptism of Christ:**[173] This painting by Aert De Gelder is self-explanatory, so please just look at the image of it below. If anyone can actually see anything in that picture that looks like anything other than a UFO, we would be amazed. The reason we say this is that it is the classic look of a flying saucer complete with a ray or beam shining down upon the earth. Even the look of the thing is metallic in nature. This painting was completed in 1710.

**The Miracle of the Snow, 1383-1440:**[174] Painted by Masolino Da Panicale, this picture hangs in the church of Santa Maria Maggiore Florence, Italy. The picture shows Mary and Joseph supposedly hovering under a circular cloud, which really doesn't look like a cloud at all. What makes it even more compelling, are all those other "clouds" that are so perfectly aligned across the entire heavens. If the painter could paint everything else so well, why do the clouds look so artificial, so unnatural, and so like UFOs? In fact, they look like a fleet of them. This is strange because there is one thing everyone can see about clouds, that they look random and even chaotic in appearance. Overall, this is a very weird, even frightening painting.

**The Annunciation, 1486.**[175] In this painting by Carlo Crivelli, we see a circular, cloud-like formation in the sky, and in the center of which is a bright light beaming down directly through a building at the recipient. Look closely at that so-called cloud in the sky. The image is highly detailed. It very closely resembles our ideas of what a UFO looks like. There is that beam of light again!

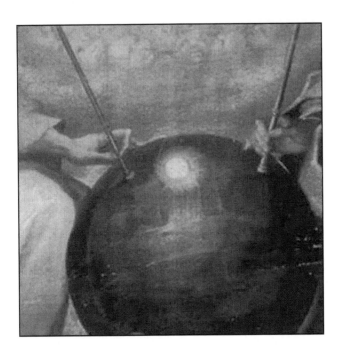

**Glorification Of The Eucharist.**[176] 1595, the artist Bona-
ventura Salimbeni painted the Glorification of the Eucharist. This
painting has caused a lot of controversy, with ancient alien proponents insisting the globe in the picture with the two long
"sticks" protruding from it looks remarkably like the old Soviet
Sputnik satellites that were lofted into space in the 1950s.

Some argue it is just meant to be either a globe of Earth, or
a celestial sphere. There are some problems with these "solutions" to the enigma of the globe in this painting. If it is meant to
be the Earth, it doesn't show any landmasses at all. If it's meant
to be a celestial sphere, why didn't the artist depict any stars on
the globe? Furthermore, why is there a reflection of light shining
on a celestial sphere? The lines on it are thought to be a celestial
grid—longitudes and latitudes, but are they? The sphere certainly
looks metallic in natures and the so-called celestial grid appears
more likely to be metal plates pounded into place.

There is also the problem of the two "sticks" protruding from the globe. Since God the Father and God the Son are holding them, some experts have argued they must be "scepters." If they are, they are the oddest portrayals of scepters we've ever come across. They are nothing like the real scepters used in that time. Additionally, they appear to be "telescoping" objects. In other words, they look collapsible onto themselves. Although telescopes were in use in this time, the concept of telescoping equipment, collapsible telescopes didn't appear until a couple of centuries later.

Let's be frank here. These "sticks" look far more like antenna than they do scepters. And if they are, where did the artist get this imagery? It would seem someone at some time must have had something like this. Likewise, what this has to do with the Holy Eucharist, which literally means "thanksgiving" and refers to celebrating the Last Supper, is a complete mystery to just about everyone.

There are more such paintings, but we just don't have room for them here. Now it's time to move on.

**Abydos Carvings:**[177] We include the picture of the Abydos carvings to show a truly ancient depiction of devices that simply didn't belong in such a time. In these carvings, one can clearly see vehicles that shouldn't have existed then. There's a picture of a helicopter, what looks remarkably like a speed or powerboat, or perhaps some sort of a UFO, as well as an airplane.

Are all these just coincidence, symbols that just accidentally look so remarkably like these things? Do they just unintentionally resemble such craft? Bizarrely, do they all end up in the same carvings by sheer chance, just coincidence, as well? We don't think so. The odds against all these "coincidences" and chances occurring would seem unlikely.

These carvings are at the Temple of Seti the First, in Abydos, Egypt. Egyptologists say these pictures just look like they do because they are plastered over older carvings, and so they ended up just looking like this by chance. Really? All those images? It's amazing how closely they resemble craft of today, and so repeatedly, if so. After all, one turning out that way might happen by sheer chance, but multiple images that so markedly seem to reflect various types of modern craft? Again, this would seem highly unlikely.

However, for those poor Egyptologists who insist on asserting this, recently, there have been some in-depth challenges to their theory, and it is just a theory of theirs and nothing more, since they've offered no proof these images were the result of plastering over.

First, opponents to their theory argue that plaster on such an important temple would have been very out of the ordinary, and most likely would not have been used at all. The Egyptians had access to special sandstone that they could use as filler, and this would most likely have been done, instead of plastering.

The idea that these were re-carved illustrations is also coming under increased attack. Again, recent experiments simply are unable to duplicate the resulting effects described by those Egyptologists.

Finally, there is the matter of the idea of the Golden Section. Various researchers state that to be able to cover over the original carvings, and still be so perfectly aligned after having done this, just seems highly unlikely, as well. Sheer chance alone would seem to dictate otherwise.

In other words, the carvings should have deviated from the idea of the Golden Section, or perfection, as Egyptians saw it. However, they do not. And when one adds to this that the resulting images don't pertain to anything else known about the Egyptians, seen repeated anywhere else…well…the evidence to support those Egyptologists who say this is just the result of re-plastering seems very unconvincing.

There is the fact of the debate itself over these carvings, as well. Never have so many Egyptologists so fiercely defended their point of view, which really is just a theory and one without any corroborating evidence. This, in itself, would make them seem highly defensive, and therefore unsure of their own assertions.

To our way of thinking, these images depict actual items that simply didn't belong in those times. Or did they? If the ancient Egyptians witnessed such things, then perhaps the ancient aliens had them. This is our contention and why we include this topic here. Megalithia would seem to have had a range of vehicles, if one judges by these images at Abydos.[178]

**The Dendera Lights:**[179] Found at the Temple of Hathor in Dendera, Egypt, are illustrations of the so-called "Dendera Lights." As with all things relating to the possibility of the ancients being more advanced than we thought, controversy surrounds these images. We're sure you've probably heard of these before, so we won't tarry on the subject here, except that we do feel it is important enough to mention, since it pertains to what we will discuss later, and that is "a retrograde civilization," which followed in the aftermath of the fall of Megalithia.

The first thing one does notice about the Temple of Hathor[180] is that it hasn't any statues or replicas of gods anywhere about it, as Egyptian temples always do. This is a strong indication that this so-called "temple" wasn't really a temple at all, at least not in the ordinary sense.

Instead, the place has a series of chambers, or "crypts" which line the eastern, southern, and western sides of the structure. Some Egyptologists argue these chambers were warehouses or places to store things for various rituals. Others say they actually were used for rituals.

Being quite small, we feel it is unlikely the chambers were employed for such purposes, since not being at all large; they could have held only a few people at any one time. What's more, this idea is also unlikely, because of how lacking in decorations the limestone walls of these crypts are, unlike the walls of the temple itself, which have many carving on them.

However, even more oddly, in a chamber or crypt underneath the temple are some rather bizarre reliefs. These inspired a whole book being written about them, titled, *"Light for the Pharaoh"* by authors Habeck and Krassa. These depictions show a large, bulb-like structure. Inside the "bulb" are a series of snakes, but very wavy ones, which closely resemble filaments in their style. These project out from the base of the "bulb" or lotus flower. There is also, what looks like a wire which travels down and around to the air god, who is kneeling on a box. Near this is a djed pillar, a power symbol, and it is connected to the "snake." Again, notice that the djed pillar is considered a "power symbol." Could this be a primitive light bulb?

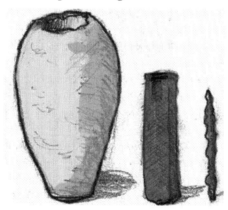

**Author: Ironie**

**Baghdad Batteries:** We have all probably heard of the "Baghdad Batteries,"[181] a number of which have been found and which are almost assuredly batteries in the real sense of the term. Combined with such a light bulb, an experiment showed that light could be produced in such a way.

Moreover, the Baghdad Batteries even predate the Egyptian Dendera carvings, so was power to operate such "bulbs" already available to the Egyptians? Moreover, if so, where did the knowledge of how to do this come from in a world so primitive that until recently, it wasn't believed they understood the concept of electricity at all, let alone know how to harness it in batteries and incandescent light bulbs?

No matter how one looks at it, the Dendera Light images are odd in the extreme. Egyptologists try to claim the bulb is actually an "aura" around the lotus flower, yet even this wouldn't explain the rest of the items in the depiction, nor does it really look like an aura at all. Check out the picture below to see for yourself and draw your own conclusion.

No, there can be little doubt. The image is that of a lamp, perhaps a rather stylized one, but then one must remember that this inner chamber of the temple was reserved for the most high-ranking priests, the so-called guardians of hidden secrets and knowledge that lesser priests were not privy too. Were these guardians trying to preserve and protect knowledge from a time long before their own? It's quite possible.

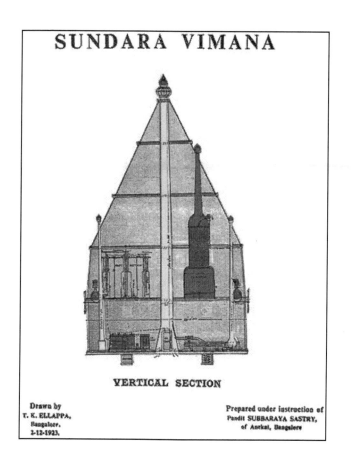

SUNDARA VIMANA

VERTICAL SECTION

Drawn by
T. K. ELLAPPA,
Bangalore,
2-12-1923.

Prepared under instruction of
Pandit SUBBARAYA SASTRY,
of Anekal, Bangalore

**Vimanas:**[182] Now as an example of alien technology, "vimanas," as they are called in the ancient Indian Vedic texts, are just about unsurpassable. So are the legends that surround them. Referred to repeatedly in various ancient Vedic texts, vimanas meant several things. "Vimana" meanings ranged from temple or palace to mythological flying machines described in Sanskrit epics.

Vimanas could be large or small. Some were described as flying palaces, and some even were said to have been flying cities. Others flew through space. According to the the Rig Veda text, considered to be one of the oldest documents known, if not the oldest, some vimanas could ride on the ground or in water. Others could operate in the air and water.

Recently vimanas have come into the limelight again for a number of reasons. The television series, *Ancient Aliens*, referred to them extensively. Their resemblance to, and their abilities to fly where and how they could, so closely resemble our modern idea of UFOs that this alone has made the subject of vimanas very popular.

**Starship Instructions:**[183] In China, several years ago, they claimed documents, ones written in ancient Sanskrit, were discovered in Lhasa, Tibet. Dr. Ruth Reyna of the University of Chandrigarth translated them. She has made the rather incredible claim that the documents contain detailed instructions for building starships, vimanas.

Professor Reyna referred to the ship's drive as based on some sort of antigravity capability. (according to the documents). She said it might loosely be compared to laghima, the mysterious force of the human ego as expressed in a person's real, physical body. She also described it as a type of "a centrifugal force," one strong enough to overcome gravity. "Laghima," by the way, is supposed to be the power that allows gurus and other holy men to levitate, to float without any visible means of doing so. They draw on this force to defy gravity. Did vimanas, as well?

Professor Reyna also referred to the vimanas as being called "astras," and they could be used to ferry people to and fro to other planets in large groups, such as would be necessary for military incursions, apparently. Dr. Reyna said that onboard these astras, the ancient Indians could have sent a detachment of men onto any world, according to the document, which is thought to be thousands of years old. Professor Reyna also said the document mentions other forces, including one that could actually increase the weight of objects.

**Vimana Discovered In Afghanistan:**[184] according to various reports, eight soldiers of the American army discovered a cave. Inside, was supposedly a 5,000-year-old vimana. Even more bizarrely, this vimana was supposed to have been trapped or deliberately placed in some sort of "time well." Whether this was on purpose or by accident, is apparently unknown.

When the soldiers tried to remove the vimana from the time well, they disappeared, quite literally. More strangely, a number of senior-level visitors from various places in America and Europe visited the area at about the same time. Oddly, some of these visits actually have been substantiated. Is this just a coincidence, or does it lend credence to the story? Whatever correlations one might draw from this must be left to the individual.

It should be mentioned that the subject of vimanas is not a new one. Perhaps the original book on the topic of ancient aliens, *Chariots of the Gods*, by Eric von Daniken, was the first really to give credence to the idea of vimanas being real, and not just things of legend. Since then, they have continually come up.

**Vimanas As Vessels of War:**[185] This last is an interesting idea, because the Vedic texts speak of battles taking place in the sky, in which vimanas were involved. These battles also took place in space, as well. According to the Vedic texts, and as we've mentioned, one even took place on the moon according to these ancient documents.

The odd part about this is that so long ago, the Indians who wrote these texts seemed to be aware of the concept of "space" and that things seen in the sky, such as the moon, were actually other worlds. Western civilization didn't arrive at similar notions until just a few centuries or so ago. The Indians seem to have been aware of this for thousands of years!

The question, of course, is how? How did they know all this so long ago? Unless, somehow, they may have been told about it or actually travelled "out there" in some way, as the servants and/or soldiers of their gods, perhaps? Did aliens use the ancient Indians as soldiers, even as the British did so many thousands of years later? It's an intriguing idea. What shock troops were storming onto other planets?

**The Vedas:**[186] As promised earlier, we wished to go into the subject of the Vedic texts, "Vedas") a little deeper, because so much of our argument about the end of Megalithia depends upon them, as well as on the Sumerian cuneiform writings.

It must be remembered that a great many of the Vedas have not been translated yet. However, two major epics have been, among others. These are the Mahabharata and the Ramayana. The version of the Mahabharata, as it is used today, apparently dates back to somewhere between 400 B.C.E. and 400 CE. However, many scholars on the subject think earlier versions of it date back many thousands of years more. Ancient Greek historians say the Indians could remember as far back as 6,000 years, and this was from their own point of view, those historians having lived around 400 B.C.E. to 500 B.C.E at Athens height of power.

The truth of this may never be known. In any case, the epic concerns events that happened long before they were written down in the Mahabharata. Prior to this, they were oral traditions handed down for countless generations, before they were codified into the epics, as we now know them. So again, they do seem to date much farther back than the modern version of the Mahabharata, which itself is about 2,500 years old give or take several centuries.

The Mahabharata is a compilation of approximately 80,000 couplets. Vyasadeva supposedly compiled these. In those couplets, vimanas are mentioned repeatedly. To summarize the Mahabharata, it is a telling of an epic war, one of considerable duration, fought between the Pandavas and the Kauravas, two hugely powerful tribes in ancient India. Very curiously, this war appears to have been at the direct instigation of the gods (ancient aliens?) The Vedas tell us they did this because the war was meant to ease the overpopulation of India at the time.

It should also be mentioned that with regard to ancient aliens, this seems to be an underlying theme, of them trying to control populations on Earth. We see this repeatedly; so much in fact, that we can't help thinking there must be something to it. As mentioned earlier, William Bramley in his book, *The Gods of Eden* drives home this point vigorously and relentlessly.

**Vimanas and the Mahabharata:**[187] In the Mahabharata, there are constant references to vimanas being used in the battles. The Mahabharata speaks of Bhima who is said to have flown "his vimana on an enormous ray, which was as brilliant as the sun and made a noise like the thunder of a storm." In addition, the epic mentions Arjuna, a warrior on the order of Gilgamesh, and tells of his ascent to heaven.

The epic specifically mentions that he is human and not a god. His trip to heaven is interesting. He is in a vehicle that shoots up to the sky making a thunderous noise as it does so. On his way, he sees other vehicles. Some have crashed. Some are simply floating stationary in the sky. Others are flying about.

The vimanas were also used to attack people in cities on the ground, but we'll get into that more under the section about the Great War that spelled the downfall for Megalithia.

**Earth Grid:**[188] Another possible technology of the Empire of Megalithia might pertain to the concept of an Earth Grid. The idea of an Earth Grid is a unique one. Hugh Newman, in his book, *The Secret Patterns of Gaia's Sacred Sites,*[189] takes a detailed look at the idea of Earth having a grid. We've spoken of this before when we mentioned ley lines.

The author stipulates that the Earth Grid, as he calls it, goes back to the beginning of Earth itself, and that many megalithic monuments were placed where they were along these ley lines in order not only to demarcate them, but to take advantage of the inherent power of the lines. Based on the theory that the Earth generates a geomagnetic effect along this "grid," the author argues that ancient civilizations understood this. They were able to utilize this power.

If this is so, it tells us something very important about Megalithia. A worldwide Empire it may have been, but many of its major structures had to be placed where they were in order for the aliens to utilize the Earth Grid power source. Therefore, although the Earth Grid was probably a boon to the aliens of Megalithia, it also restricted them. It required them to place their structures in highly specific locations.

This limited them in that regard. Therefore, the ancient aliens were definitely not all-powerful. They, like us, seem to have circumscribed powers. They weren't capable of doing anything and everything they wanted. They had limitations.

There are other technologies, but these were the main ones we wished to cover here. This was in order to give you a good grounding, a clear idea of the technological capabilities of Megalithia. Next, we'll discuss the aliens themselves, as to whether or not there was more than one type of them, how they may have looked, and what motivated them.

# Chapter 13

## Ancient Alien Races

**E**xactly who were these aliens that ruled humanity in that first Empire on Earth? Well, we don't have any photographs of them, of course, but we do have other sources that might provide us with images of them.[190] Sources for such images include, but are not limited to, bass reliefs, carved depictions, statues, and other artifacts. However, not all these images agree with each other. There may be good reason for this.

In addition, as another source, we have the legends and myths of various cultures around the world, with reference to their particular idea of the sky gods, or sky guardians. Are such legends a reliable source? Well, if we based all of our assumptions on just one particular legend of one particular culture, no, probably not. Nevertheless, if we take them as a whole, sifted them for similarities, we may be able to come up with some general ideas of what the aliens may have looked like.

For instance, the Hopi Indians often have their Kachina gods sporting elaborate feathered outfits. The god, Quetzalcoatl, of the Aztecs, or Kukulkan among the Yucatec Maya, was supposed to been a feathered serpent. Even the sky guardians of the Sumerians were shown in depictions often as having feathered wings.

Is this all just mere coincidence? No, we don't think so. The idea of feathered beings from the sky, strange creatures, just appears too often in many highly diverse cultures from around the world. Therefore, it is likely some of the aliens may have had some type of feathered wings and/or were reptilian, or serpent-like in nature into the bargain.[191]

Again, William Bramley delves heavily into the serpent aspect of the entire history of our civilization. He even speaks of a clandestine Brotherhood of the Snake that dates back thousands of years.[192]

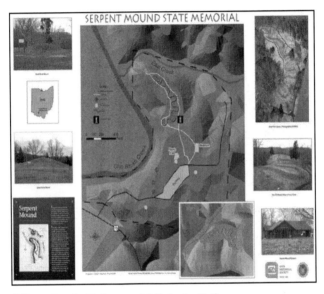

**Timothy A. Price and Nichole I. Stump**

**The Serpent Mound in Ohio:** This serpent-shaped mound reflects the major points of the Constellation of Draco in its construction. The purpose for these mounds is a complete mystery. The effort in creating them must have been prodigious!

As a curious addition to this whole snake business, there are "serpent" mounds, not only in the United States, but also in Scotland and Ontario, although the one in Ohio is easily the world's largest.[193] The Ohio serpent mound is located in an odd area. It is on the rim of an ancient meteor crater, a large one. The area is known for magnetic anomalies, as well. So why here? Was this just chance?

Why would ancient peoples of North America build the world's largest snake mound accurately to reflect the constellation of Draco? How did they know they were on the rim of a huge and ancient crater, one that today just looks like a very large, but natural valley? Were they aware of the magnetic "anomalies" of the area, as well?

Finally, why is it that one can only really see the mound from a great height? Park officials have built a tall tower (many stairs!) so people can climb it and see the snake mound as it should be seen—from high up. This is very reminiscent of the Lines of Nazca, which also require a great height to view them, as they should be seen—from above.

**Angels as Aliens:**[194] With regard to winged aliens, angels often have been illustrated as being human-like, but with wings. Throughout the Old Testament of the Bible, angels were considered messengers of God. Their appearance often meant life-altering events were about to occur.

Many Ancient Alien theorists believe that angels were actually aliens themselves. The fact angels are so similar in appearance to pictures of the Anunnaki, may be more than just coincidence, though. However, the idea of feathered and/or winged beings seems to permeate the cultures of the Earth, with roots in vocal histories that date back to the very beginnings of such civilizations.

According to the Vedic texts, there were many alien races. In addition, even these may have changed from time to time. If Earth was a place of resources, there may have been more than one race vying for dominion of it. Furthermore, different races could well have controlled different areas of the planet. And if there were battles and wars, as we believe, then which races may have been resident on earth at any particular time may have changed on a regular basis. There would be winners and losers, with the losers kicked off planet.

This would mean the images of such races passed down to us would differ, depending on their place of origin and when created. This actually does seem to be the case. Below, are some of these:

**Ancient Sumerians:**[195] The ancient Sumerians had various images of the sky gods. One type shows a being with an elongated skull, pronounced shoulders, and wide slit-like eyes set at sharp angles to the nose and mouth. Another type of common portrayal shows creatures with an almost heart-shaped head, with large bulging eyes. The third type of depiction shows human-like creatures, but again, sporting those feathered wings.

The Anunnaki, by all accounts, also had creatures who were "not alive," according to cuneiform writings. There has been a great deal of conjecture of just what these creatures looked like. Supposedly, the Anunnaki created them. Furthermore, the Anunnaki, if you remember, were supposed to have created humans, as well, and supposedly made us to look like them to some degree.

**Temehea Tohua, Statues of an Alien Race:**[196] Temehea Tohua is on Nucu Hiva, the largest island of the Marquesas in French Polynesia. Here, there is a very bizarre group of statues. The main features of these are being overly large and elongated heads. The eyes are oversized. The mouth is also overly large. The bodies, by comparison, are small.

There is a generally reptilian look to the creatures, or even amphibian. The heads tilt up, as if looking into the sky, in a very similar pose to the statues of Easter Island. There are also statues of creatures with small bodies, oversized heads, and wide, bugging eyes. Although similar in appearance to the other statues, they are distinctly different, as well.

**Ancient Gods with Human-Like Appearance:**[197] Among the various civilizations of the world are various pantheons of gods who were remarkably human in their characteristics and looks, except for the powers they wielded. Whether the Norse, Greek,[198] or Roman gods, for instance, this seems to be a common thread.

As with almost all such pantheons, the gods supposedly created humans to resemble themselves. Could this have actually been so? Well, when combined with the story of the Sumerian Anunnaki, and the claim they made humans to mine gold for them, and created them in their own image, one can see where this theme does keep repeating. Then, of course, the Bible says much the same thing, that man was created in God's image.

Are all these myths and legends just that and nothing more? Are they mere stories made up so very long ago? Alternatively, are all these creation stories grounded in something more real, the idea that a race of powerful beings did create humans, and created us to look very much like themselves?

The idea all these disparate civilizations, separated geographically and by time, just being so coincidental in their religious beliefs and creation stories, seems a little overwhelming to us. We feel there may well be some truth to the idea. So many cultures believed so deeply this was true. A few might be a coincidence, but repeatedly around the world, there is this concept of powerful creatures coming down from the sky and creating humanity, often in their own image.

Why do we speak of this here? Well, if we were a race created in the image of another, then the reverse is also true. There must have been a race of beings that look very much like us. So not only are their feathered serpents, reptiles, amphibious beings with large heads and small bodies, elongated skulls, etc., but there must have been a species who closely resembled humans, too. This means there must have been multiple races Whether they all came to Earth at the same time, or at different times, is a question. Nevertheless, the Vedic texts state there were numerous alien species and they often warred with each other.

**Chapter Conclusion:** It would appear some alien races were veritable monstrosities to us. Others were humanoid in form, and still others looked very human. Moreover, if we go by the ancient texts of India, we realize that not only did the aliens look very different from each other, but also for whatever reasons, they didn't seem to get along very well.

The Empire of Megalithia, it seems, was often in a state where the rulers were at each other's throats, literally and figuratively. Therefore, not only do we get an idea of how the aliens may have looked, but we also get a good idea of how they behaved.

Where did they come from? It's not enough to say that they just came from "out there." Is there anything more we can discover about their possible origins? In the next chapter, we will try to arrive at some conclusions regarding this.

# Chapter 14

## Possible Origins of the Aliens

Exactly where did the aliens come from? We'd all like to know the answer to that. We do have some clues. Certain constellations have always figured prominently in the cultures of various civilizations. The Egyptians seem to have had a "real thing" for the Orion Belt. The Pleiades also are prominent with them and in certain other civilizations.[199] The constellation Taurus is yet another one. The constellations of Draco and Cygnus, as well as the stars Zeta Reticuli[200] and Sirius[201] are also included, among others.

When we say these constellations were significant to ancient civilizations, we mean exactly that. Major effort was made to build structures such as the pyramids of Giza, either to emulate the constellations above them in the heavens, or to point to them in some way. It is interesting to note that many of these ancient structures were at their best alignment with those constellations at approximately 10,000 to 12,000 years ago. Another indication of the time of Megalithia?

Why would the civilizations go to such enormous effort and lengths to build such giant structures in such a way, if those particular constellations were not important to them? Moreover, if they were so important, just why were they?

Yes, some of the constellations are prominent in the heavens, but others not nearly so much. So if the argument can be made that the structures are related to the most conspicuous star patterns in the skies, why then did some put forth such effort to create some buildings that emulated constellations that weren't nearly so dominate?

The answer would appear to be that certain constellations held powerful meaning to those ancient civilizations. This must be so, or they wouldn't have invested so much time and effort, as well as capital expenditure, to create such structures.

**Zeta Reticuli:** Another possible origin of some of the aliens might be from the star system, Zeta Reticuli. The star system is approximately 39 light years from Earth. This particular system first achieved notoriety in the 1960s. A married couple, Barney and Betty Hill,[202] claim to have been abducted. The abduction, the details of which came out under hypnosis, was supposed to have been perpetrated by aliens. The story, *The Interrupted Journey*, became a bestseller in 1966, as well as then being adapted as a made-for-television movie. Both Mr. and Mrs. Hill claim the events were real. They also drew a star map. Later, it was determined the map most likely showed the star system of Zeta Reticuli.

We mention this incident here, because many UFO adherents believe this is where one type of species of aliens came from, Zeta Reticuli. It may well be that if this is true, such aliens, commonly known as the "Grays," may have been here a very long time, indeed, or have visited us before, perhaps millennia ago. To put it another way, the Grays may not be new arrivals on Earth.[203] They might have been part of the alien oligarchy of Megalithia.

Also according to UFO adherents, the reptilian-looking species of aliens may have originated from the star system of Alpha Draconis. The star system is located in the night sky between the constellations of Ursa Major and Ursa Minor. This star system is approximately 215 light years from Earth.

UFO adherents think the reptilian aliens are coming to earth even now, so again, they could've been here in the far past, too. Were they another alien race of Megalithia? It's distinctly possible, considering the ancient images we have of reptilian creatures.

If the idea of reptilian aliens seems far-fetched, think about all the images painted in our own Western civilization. For instance, our image of Satan, the devil, is of a very reptilian looking creature, often complete with bat wings and a tail. Genesis even described Satan as being a serpent.

Besides this, we have many other statues and pictures of reptilian creatures. Gargoyles, those hideous stone monsters that top the cornices of many a church in Europe, look distinctly reptilian, complete with their bat-like wings. Traditional images of the incubus are also reptilian.

The history of our civilization abounds with such types of images and statues. Why is there this recurring theme, incredible similarities in each of these types of interpretations throughout the ages? Might not there be a common origin for them, a real creature that once visited the Earth? Might we now remember the aliens as mythological creatures, monsters of legend, such as trolls, gnomes, fairies, leprechauns, sprites, and other such beings?

Before you dismiss this idea out of hand, remember that every culture on earth has legends and myths of these types of beings. Whether Ireland with its leprechauns, England with its fairies, Europe with its trolls, all cultures seem to have some type of supernatural creatures in their legends. In fact, all cultures have legends with such sorts of creatures to varying degrees. If there is no basis in fact at all for them, then why do they exist at all? Why are they so prevalent around the globe? As mentioned, the Anunnaki were said even to have non-living creatures to help pilot their vessels and to work for them. Could this be where the legends of golems, zombies, or even the undead originated?

Again, please remember that for many of these cultures these aren't legends. They believe these things are true and just as firmly as we believe in the Bible, the Torah, or the Koran.

# PART 5
# THE DECLINE AND FALL OF MEGALITHIA

# Chapter 15

# The Beginning of the End of Megalithia

Nothing lasts forever and neither did Megalithia. The Empire couldn't last, although it may have existed for an incredibly long time. As mentioned in the prior chapters, there are probably a number of reasons for the demise of Megalithia. We'll discuss the most likely ones here in more depth.

**Too Many Alien Species:** First, there is the matter of the number of different types of alien species. The Vedas say there were (and may still be) 400,000 different types of humans and subhumans. Aliens were also considered part of this 400,000. The species were divided into three main groups, the divine, semi-divine, and human. The divine are easy enough to categorize, because they were the true aliens. The same goes for the human category, since they were (are) us. It is the semi-divine where things become vaguer.

Many cultures, including the Sumerians, Hopi, Navajo, Mayans, Aztecs, and even those of Europe and Asia, talk about the divine (aliens?), interbreeding on occasion with human women.[204] The result was such semi-divine characters as Gilgamesh, Hercules, and many, many others. These then would be part of the semi-divine group. There attributes often included some extra powers normal humans did not possess, such as great strength and longevity.

Angels, as we now call them, and which comes from the

root word "messenger," may also have been part of this group. These were beings, who if not true aliens, acted on their behalf as messengers to humans. They might have also acted as warriors for the aliens, as well. When we use the term "angels," we don't mean them in the modern sense, but rather as servants and messengers for alien races.

The references to non-living servants of the gods (aliens) may refer to androids, robots, clones, or such. The texts are unclear on their exact nature, other than they were nonliving and that they were servants.

How could there be so many types of aliens. Well, for example, the precepts of Hinduism are definite with regard to there being an infinite number of planets, solar systems, and even other universes (parallel?) to our own.

Bharadwaja, an ancient sage who lived some three thousand years ago, categorized the alien vimanas or flying machines into three main types. The one of interest to us here in this section is the type that can travel to other star systems and/or even other universes. The truly remarkable thing about this and it is something that certainly mystifies scientists of today, is that Bharadwaja should have so clearly set out these different types of vessels.

Why is this mystifying? Because they clearly demonstrate that humans knew of other worlds, star systems, and even other universes over three thousand years ago! This is incredible. However, the reason we mention this here, is to show the possibly inconceivable number of aliens there may be, and that many may have been here in the time of Megalithia.

Therefore, the top tier of Megalithian society, the aliens, could well have been varied, with many species not interacting well with others, having different agendas, and different methods of how to go about obtaining their goals. It seems they most likely didn't always "just get along."

What did all this mean for Megalithia? Well, at the very least, it was probably a major balancing act to maintain peace and stability among the various races of aliens under such circumstances. According to the Vedic texts, this effort failed on a regular basis, and finally in a big way, seemingly once and for all.

Consequently, this matter of multiple alien races was probably the biggest single issue. Worse, there were different factions within the same species, as well as quarrels and battles between completely different species, according to those texts.

Again, it may well have been that not only did different alien species rule different regions of the world, but so might have different factions of the same species, as well. In other words, Megalithia probably was not a monolithic empire, but more like a series of colonies ruled by various species. The setup might have been similar to the way the European countries all had colonies in Africa, and fought and bickered with each other over them.

Even so, from humanity's perspective, this wouldn't have changed things much for them in their daily lives, the human's lot in life in those ancient days. Aliens may have squabbled among each other, even as the European powers did in the 19th Century, but as those same European countries did with Africa, the aliens still jointly ruled virtually all of the Earth.

One more argument here and that is as mentioned earlier, because of the extreme duration of Megalithia, some aliens may have gained ascendancy even as other species went into decline. In such a highly competitive style of civilization, this would seem to be just as likely then, as it is for modern nation states of today, who experience the same rise and fall in fortunes. For practical purposes, then, it may well have been different species came and went over time, but the battles for control went on all the time.

However, just as that vast coalition of powers eventually fell into conflict with each other in Europe, and resulted in two devastating world wars, we think the aliens did the same thing. Whether this conflict originated on Earth, was something that just simmered over the centuries here, or came from "out there," we can't be sure.

Was there a clash of alien civilizations among the stars? Was Earth just a colonial backwater of a planet that became involved in some vast interstellar conflict? If one goes by the Vedas, the source of the conflicts and disagreements did come from "out there."

We do have one caveat here, though. If there were different alien races upon the Earth, and they governed different regions autonomously, one would have thought there would be a more diverse look to the megalithic ruins of different areas of our planet. Although there are some variations in the types of structures built, overall, there seems to be more that is similar than different in these structures.

Therefore, it may be Earth was ruled by one type of aliens, but they were at odds with other alien races "out there." This would seem to be in accordance with the Vedic texts, as well. However, if we're to go by those, as well as the Sumerian ones, then we have to assume that there were problems between members of the same species, too, factions who apparently had control of certain regions and/or peoples, as in India, for example. We think this because the texts mention what appear to have been a series of brushfire wars, where the aliens controlling various human tribes, fought each other by proxy.

Still, something must have happened in the final days of Megalithia. As dissension among the aliens grew and as battles began to take place, at first limited to mere skirmishes, but later, major battles, it seems humanity, whether it willed it or no, became increasingly involved. Again, the Vedic texts speak of armies of various tribes attacking each other in the name of their respective gods/aliens, at their very instigation. They were also assisted with weaponry and vehicles by those same aliens in their conflicts. In other words, a war was fight by proxy amongst the aliens.

**Too Many People:** A second major problem for the Empire of Megalithia was the human population. Again, we refer to the Vedic texts. They are a rich source of information about those ancient times, it seems, and they refer to a problem with the growth in the human population of that period.

To put it none too politely, by the aliens' standards, it

would appear we bred like flies. Whether as the Sumerian cuneiform writings say, we were created by the aliens, or whether we were already here and/or altered, is a moot point as far as this goes. At least, it is as far as how fast we managed to breed, and how quickly our population grew.

The Vedic state, quite clearly, that the aliens started wars just to help reduce the surplus population of India and by extension, probably the world. This is an overwhelming idea in itself, because those texts are very old. They speak of a time even earlier, when India's population was already too high?

The aliens saw this as a threat according to the texts. One can see why, if they were slow breeders by comparison. Crowd control would have been increasingly difficult, as those crowds grew larger and larger. The Sumerian cuneiform writings also speak of something similar.

There would have been a tipping point, when the alien colonial authorities simply couldn't control the mobs, if the size of the mobs kept growing. Mutinies, as with the Great Mutiny in India against the British colonial authorities there, would probably have occurred. Rebellions undoubtedly were an issue with the aliens. So not only were the aliens fighting among themselves, and perhaps with other species of aliens, but they all faced the problem of a growing human presence on the planet.

Tension over time must have steadily increased. Fear of the humans must have steadily grown. Again, In William Bramley's book, *The Gods of Eden*, he constantly and repeatedly stresses how aliens kept trying to control humanity's spread across the world. He specifically makes a strong case that plagues, and what we now think of as having been ancient natural catastrophes, were actually practical measures invoked by the aliens to reduce the number of humans on this planet.

**Change in Status Quo:** A final major problem for the aliens might have been another change in the status quo, as well. Even if they had managed a long-term balancing act between each other on the Earth, events in space may have gone differently. There is evidence, according to the texts, that something "out there" changed dramatically. Based on the Vedas, a major war started. It was an interstellar one. Megalithia's days were now inevitably numbered....

# Chapter 16

## The Great War of Megalithia

**A**ll good things must come to an end, and so, too, must bad things, as well. Megalithia, which may have been in a long decline already, had now reached the tipping point. Things swiftly worsened. Those same texts speak of aliens in flying machines now directly participating in the battles. The Vedas speak of how flying vimanas attacked the armies and homeland cities of the human Vrishis and Andhakas tribes. Here is a direct quote from the Mahabharata:

> *"Gurkha flying in his swift and powerful Vimana hurled against the three cities of the Vrishnis and Andhakas a single projectile charged with all the power of the Universe. An incandescent column of smoke and fire, as brilliant as ten thousands suns, rose in all its splendor. It was the unknown weapon, the Iron Thunderbolt, a gigantic messenger of death which reduced to ashes the entire race of the Vrishnis and Andhakas."*

This is one of many such verses on the subject in the texts of the Ramayana and Mahabharata. There are many more, but the above suffices for our purposes. And don't forget the war instigated between the Pandavas and the Kauravas, as well. Everyone, it seemed, was going to war.

The Sumerian cuneiform texts also refer to disagreements among the gods, and go on to talk about a great human rebellion, as well. This is interesting. Whereas, normally, humans probably would have had little chance of successfully rebelling against such powerful masters, in the midst of a war amongst themselves, the aliens might have been at a distinct disadvantage if such should have happened. Humanity, or at least some of it, saw an opportunity and seized it, according to the Sumerian texts.

As the quote by Abraham Lincoln says, "A house divided against itself, cannot stand." The aliens "house" finally didn't stand either. The walls of that house were beaten at from without by other aliens, and from within by their own one-time servants. Whatever the exact details were, it seems humanity finally won free of its otherworld masters, one way, or the other. Still, the results would be dire for humanity, as we shall see in the next chapter.

Nevertheless, the Empire didn't go with a whimper but rather a bang, and a big one at that. Again, we have but to refer to the translations of the cuneiform texts about the Anunnaki to know dissension towards the end of their reign was apparently rife. The Vedic texts also tell us this.

Although they differ in details and just how detailed their explanations are, they both say very much the same thing. The aliens began fighting with each other. War ultimately broke out, a worldwide one. Rebellions ensued.

But what kind of war? Was it limited in scope, or no holds barred? Well, we think from the evidence we've garnered, it was more of the no-holds-barred variety. Why do we believe this? Because we feel there is plausible evidence that it was a thermonuclear war,[205] among other things.

Besides nukes, there are references to some type of beam weaponry that may have been used in the battles, as well. If one goes by the Vedic texts alone, the war wasn't just limited to Earth, but was simultaneously fought in space, and even on our moon, as we mentioned earlier. Here is another quotation from the Mahabharata and we've interjected [in brackets] what various comments probably mean in modern terms:

> "When the weapon, a blazing missile of smokeless fire is unleashed; dense arrows of flame, like a great shower, issued forth upon creation, encompassing the enemy... A thick gloom swiftly settled upon the Pandava hosts. All points of the compass were lost in darkness [nuclear winter?]. Fierce winds began to blow [shock wave and blast effects?]. Clouds roared upward [mushroom cloud from atomic explosion?], showering dust and gravel [fallout?]. Birds choked madly... the very elements seemed disturbed. The sun seemed to waver in the heavens. The earth shook, scorched by the terrible violent heat of this weapon [effects of a "thermonuclear" blast?]. Elephants burst into flame [horribly, this happened with people at Hiroshima and Nagasaki] and ran to and fro in a frenzy...

*over a vast area, other animals crumpled to the ground and died. From all points of the compass the arrows of flame rained continuously and fiercely."*[206] [Firestorm?]

Doesn't that sound eerily reminiscent of a thermonuclear device? Oddly, there is reference to a weapon used by the gods (aliens) that is forbidden because it is so terrible. Was this an ancient attempt to "ban the bomb?"[207] Was using nukes even going too far for aliens?

This following passage seems absolutely to describe the effects of a thermonuclear blast. It is a description of an explosion like "ten thousand suns:"

*"The corpses were so burnt they were no longer recognizable. Hair and nails fell out. Pottery broke without cause... After a few hours all foodstuffs were infected...."*[208]

That description is identical to exactly what happens when people suffer from radiation sickness. Their hair and nails fall out. They lose their eyesight. Their skin cracks and bleeds as the cells in their body die. Even the part about foodstuffs is accurate. Foodstuffs become contaminated by radiation.

What did the soldiers do to attempt to avoid this fate?

*...to escape from this fire the soldiers threw themselves in streams to wash themselves and their equipment."*

What is the first thing we do when someone has been dusted with fallout? Why, we tell them to shower themselves thoroughly, wash every part of their body, just as those soldiers did in ancient times. What's more, we do the same with all equipment. All must be cleansed of any radioactive particles. Water is how we go about this cleansing.

Furthermore, it has been estimated that half a million people could have died in that one blast. It was about the size of those that devastated Japan in 1945. Archeologist Francis Taylor stated that etchings in some nearby temples he translated, suggested the people prayed to be spared from the "great light" that was coming to lay ruin to their city.

When we consider that the Mahabharata is just supposed to be the stuff of legends, it seems amazingly coincidental that it describes a thermonuclear blast, all the details of it, and the aftermath, as well as the effects of radiation poisoning on people, and all so clearly, so vividly, and so precisely. Can all this just be coincidence? We hardly think so! Somebody, thousands of years ago, was describing a thermonuclear war. Moreover, it wasn't just the one blast, either. There is other evidence.

**Mohenjo-Daro and Harappa:** Both these ancient cities show ancient signs of having undergone some sort of nuclear attack. In the archeological digs, at an ancient street level, were discovered skeletons. In some cases, the skeletons appeared to have been dropped in their tracks, as if attempting to flee, and were still holding hands. Death struck them very swiftly. The bones, in some cases, were found to be 50 times higher in radioactive levels compared to the natural surrounding background level of the general area today.

Also, vitrified pieces of pottery (clay that has undergone such intense heat the material turns to a form of glass—this was first discovered after atomic blasts sites in New Mexico were inspected where sand there was vitrified), were also found in the digs. They also found remains of an ancient crater, but no meteor pieces. The side of the wall facing the blast crater had undergone vitrification, but not the other side. Furthermore, both cities appeared to have been destroyed at about the same time.

In the vicinity of Rajasthan (India,) near Jodhpur, there is a three-square-mile area of radioactive ash. People living in this area suffer a markedly higher rate of cancer, as well as birth defects. The Indian authorities banned access to the zone recently when radiation levels unaccountably went very high.

As if this isn't enough evidence, a town was unearthed dating back 8,000 to 12,000 years ago, and it, too, contains evidence it may have been wiped out by a thermonuclear blast.[209] An ancient city was unearthed, as well, which the evidence indicates was the victim of an atomic explosion some 8,000 to 12,000 years ago.

There is even more evidence. There are remains of vitrified fortresses in Scotland, Ireland, and Northern Europe, including Germany. The stones of these fortresses show they've been subjected to intense heat to the point of vitrification. Supporting the idea further is the fort itself was the object of this heat. The same stone, naturally formed in the surrounding region, doesn't show any signs of vitrification.

We'll say once more, it takes the heat of an asteroid impact or thermonuclear blast to cause vitrification. It's not easy turning stone to glass. Volcanoes can manage it, but there is none in these areas, active or otherwise, that could account for this. Nor would volcanoes be so selective in what they destroyed.

For less tangible forms of evidence, we can look to various sources, including the Bible. In the Old Testament, we have the story of Sodom and Gomorrah being destroyed by a rain of fire from the sky. Then there are legends, as well. Atlantis, we are told, was destroyed in just a day and its ruins sank beneath the waves.

We also have all the various myths about the gods of different civilizations around the world. In almost every single case, the gods underwent a great battle. The Norse gods were not only teachers of humans, but fierce warriors, as well, and legends say they literally blazed across the sky in shining chariots (UFOs?). They had weapons of such power they could even destroy mountains. Thor, Odin, and Frey, among others had such powers at their disposal.

Ultimately, they fought the battle referred to as Gotter-dammerung, the "Twilight of the Gods," and this brought them down, destroyed Valhalla, their sacred place of residence. The Greek gods of Olympus fought the Titans in a similar sort of battle, but in this version, they won, at great cost.

There are many more such examples, but we won't go into them here. We just wanted to give you some general idea of the extent of the warfare involved, and the area it might have encompassed. If these legends have any basis in fact at all, and there are such myths around the world, then the final battle of Megalithia was awesome, indeed, perhaps even bringing down "mountains."

Based on all this, it would appear the war was a brutal one, and fought far and wide, even in space, as well, if one believes the Vedas are an actual recounting of that war. The devastation wreaked upon Megalithia must have been enormous.

According to the above information, entire cities were destroyed, their populations wiped out. This, despite their praying to be spared the consequences of the "great light." They annihilated entire armies. Aliens destroyed each other's vimanas and themselves. Megalithia was stricken unto death. What little of it that may have survived, was to face even more catastrophes.

# Chapter 17

## Climate Change, Mega-fauna, and the Great Flood

It has been said, according to some studies, that even a small regional nuclear war could create a nuclear winter that might last up to ten years in length.[210] If this is even close to being true, and we have no reason to doubt it, then imagine what a nuclear war on the scale of the one that destroyed Megalithia must have caused. Moreover, it wasn't the only thing to do damage.

# NEW THEORIES

**The Great Flood:** We have developed our own theory, based on the available evidence, that something else occurred, something else that was momentous as a consequence of the war. We think it's no accident that the last Ice Age was ending at about the time Megalithia did, except for one major resurgence, and that was the Younger Dryas Period.

We'll get to that in just a bit. First, we wish to discuss the Great Flood. The evidence of so many coastal cities now being under water, and many of them dating back to the time of Megalithia, would seem to suggest that sea levels had to have risen at the same time Megalithia was dying, and suddenly, if only in the form of tsunamis.

Was this deliberate? Did the aliens use their beam weaponry

and nuclear bombs to trigger a meltdown of the ice fields, speeding up the whole process? Certainly, there is ample evidence to believe the Ice Age was coming to an end on its own, but did the war do something to precipitate a sudden increase in this happening, if only temporarily?

If Megalithia was principally an empire of coastal towns, as seems to be the case, did the aliens create the Great Flood further to decimate their opponents' bases? Is this where the legend of the Great Flood comes from?

Remember, almost every culture in the world has some kind of legend of the Great Flood. Could this event have been the origin of those legends? After all, something must account for all those drowned cities and towns. When one looks at the dates of the demise of some of the cities, when they existed, it puts many of them right at the time of the Megalithian Empire. In addition, many legends say these cities drowned very quickly, "overnight," as some stories say. Therefore, whatever happened was swift.

**Mastodons and Woolly Mammoths:**[211] Wooly Mammoths, mastodons, giant beavers, ground sloths, and perhaps even saber-toothed cats all became extinct sometime near the time of the demise of Megalithia, and yet they thrived during the time of the existence of the Empire.

Then, abruptly and mysteriously, they disappeared.[212] Some scientist tried to argue humans caused their extinction, but this has since been largely discounted. Humans had been present for some time already in North America and yet these animal populations stayed relatively stable for long periods during that time of coexistence. Furthermore, very little evidence has been found to suppose that the diet of the early North Americans relied to any real extent on such animals. Bones of other animals have been found aplenty in caves and at campsites, but not much evidence was found of these much larger creatures making meals for those primitives.

Besides, practically speaking, it would have been far easier for those ancient humans to kill an elk or deer, rather than to take on a giant mastodon or fearsome saber-tooth tiger. No, the mega fauna had relatively stable populations. Then, quite precipitously, they all became extinct.

Either humans of the time suddenly were selectively trying to fight the worst animals imaginable in their environment, or something else killed those creatures. Something else must have wiped out all those different and large species of creatures.

That something could have been a thermonuclear war, or its aftermath of a nuclear winter. Perhaps, both of them combined, are instrumental in the giants' demise. One thing we do know these days, and that is during times of great stress, larger species are more likely to suffer the most and become extinct. Smaller species can more easily find shelter in burrows in the ground and require less food to sustain themselves. They also are usually faster and more prolific breeders than larger animals. This means their ability to recover from such an event as a thermonuclear war or nuclear winter would progress more rapidly and be more likely to occur.

**Asteroids as Kinetic Weapons:**[213] Another weapon might have been used by the aliens in their war against each other. That is, they may have used asteroids as kinetic weapons. Small asteroids, aimed precisely, and given the correct speed, could be sent on their way towards earth. Their place of impact could even be precisely computed. The result could be small asteroid impacts in various oceans causing tsunamis around the adjacent coastal regions. Alternatively, they could be used on land or over it, as either impacting bombs or airburst-style blasts.

The effect of too many of these would be the same as with thermonuclear explosions—that is, a nuclear winter. Using asteroids on their own, or in conjunction with nukes, could have had a devastating effect on the Earth.

If one has capable spacecraft, asteroids would make a marvelous weapon. They are cheap and easy to use. The right nudge at the right time would send them hurtling out of orbit and on their way. Even today, we're discussing moving a small (very small) asteroid into an orbit around the moon to be used as sort of a base, and to better understand how asteroids came to be, and what they may be composed of.

If we can manage this, then surely more advanced species could do even better than we could. Some ancient alien theorists even claim that aliens might have wiped out the dinosaurs, and either used thermonuclear devices to do it, or an asteroid, or both. By one estimate, about half of the remaining dinosaurs died in the asteroid explosion alone.

Therefore, perhaps it was an asteroid airburst or multiple ones over North America that caused the crown fires and decimated the mega-fauna population of that continent. The use of asteroids as kinetic weapons would also explain the flooding of large coastal areas, and the changing of the geography along those coastal regions. Legends of the Great Flood may come from just that, the use of asteroids as bombs.

**The Younger Dryas a Nuclear Winter:** The Big Freeze, as The Younger Dryas stadial is sometimes called, was of relatively short duration, but it was intense. It lasted only for about 1,300 years, give or take about 70 years. It supposedly occurred about 12,800 years ago to 11,500[214] years ago. Despite a general trend towards warming conditions, the Dryas periods, with the Older Dryas stadial lasting about 300 years, and the Younger Dryas lasting four times longer, marked times of extreme cold.

With regard to the Younger Dryas, there is evidence of their having been continent-wide forest fires in North America, crown fires, as we mentioned earlier. Some scientists claim this was the result of an asteroid impact or fragments of an asteroid striking in what is known as an "airburst" over North America. The Tunguska Blast of 1908 was such an airburst. This would have been a much larger one, and would have caused the fires, and the resulting nuclear-style winter.

However many scientists refute this idea, saying there is little or no evidence to support such a contention as the cause being an asteroid. They point that no fragments of such an asteroid have been found, and unlike the Tunguska Blast, which destroyed whatever it was that exploded, such a larger asteroid should have left some fragments, even as the meteor over Russia recently did, although also an airburst.

They further state that the dating of the event could be off, that the dating of the ash layer was imprecise. If so, this means the event could easily have occurred at the end time of Megalithia and may well have. In any case, our timing of the end of Megalithia, as was clearly stated at the outset of this book, is by necessity, somewhat fluid. The timespan for it could stretch as much as 1000 to 1,500 years either way.

So it could well be that this 1,300 year "Big Freeze," The Younger Dryas, could have been a nuclear winter caused by the thermonuclear war that ended Megalithia. Even the ash layer in North America could be a result of the crown fired caused by this war, the result of multiple nuclear strikes and/or smaller kinetic-weapon asteroids.

This means that not only did the ending of Megalithia bring about the destruction of the Empire itself, but it may have caused the Great Flood, thus the submerging of multiple coastal towns and villages. There would have been the thermonuclear war, as well, one that has left its mark to this day, with remnants of radiation still around. Even a nuclear winter may have followed that lasted for 1,200 to 1300 years.

**Chapter Conclusion:** Based on the above items occurring,

here is the sequence of events for the final war of Megalithia:

**1.** Political events among the alien species deteriorate to the point of brushfire wars coalescing into a major one. What were scattered conflicts grew in size and severity.

**2.** Human population pressures (compared to the number of aliens in residence on the planet) begin to allow humanity to resist and even rebel against their alien masters.

**3.** The war swiftly turns into a major conflagration, meaning all types of available weapons are then put to use. These include atomic bombs, but also beam weaponry and possibly asteroids as kinetic weapons.

**4.** The war either spreads from Earth to space, even from interstellar space, or perhaps the reverse is true, and the war came to us from "out there." Some evidence points to this last being the case.

**5.** Humans were aware of the power of their masters, and their weaponry. As mentioned in the Vedas, people even prayed to be spared the "great light," of an atomic bomb flash.

**6.** The war decimate the aliens and even more so, the earthbound humans of the time.

**7.** Climatic changes on a major scale ensue. Atomic bombs/kinetic weapons cause crown fires, as in North America. Perhaps, simply the sheer number of nukes used resulted in the ice sheets partially melting, at least temporarily, at a faster rate. Alternatively, perhaps large meteors or small asteroids were lobbed into the oceans to create tsunamis.

Either way, the coastal regions, the main areas of Megalithia, became inundated. The geography of coastal zones changed, with some regions being permanently flooded. Cities drowned swiftly, sank beneath the waves. This all happened very quickly, on a short time scale.

**8.** The aftermath of the war was a prolonged nuclear winter, and a severe one. Today, we refer to that nuclear winter as the Younger Dryas.

**9.** Wooly mammoths, mastodons, saber-toothed tigers, giant sloths, and other mega-fauna couldn't survive the combination of the war and the resulting nuclear winter. Species went extinct. The last of the giant land animals were gone forever.

**10.** Human populations, not nearly as high as they are today (although high enough to have threatened the colonial aliens on Earth), plunged, as the atomic war wreaked its havoc on the few population centers.

Now, having seen what the war did, what were the long-term after effects? We assure you, they were many, and they were severe. The consequences were also felt long into the future. Moreover, they would fundamentally change the nature of civilization for humanity. However, this would be a while in coming. First, the human race would have to recover from the devastation of the collapse of the Megalithian Empire.

Exactly what did these consequences entail? Well, they were many and varied and not just for the people of Earth. The aliens, too, suffered devastating consequences. The planet itself also suffered.

There is the question of what happened to those alien races, as well. There is also the question of how humanity survived. In our final chapters, we will discuss the results of the downfall of Megalithia, what happened to the aliens, and humanity.

We will also discuss what might be in store for us in the future. Why is this last important? Well, we can't simply assume the aliens all left the Earth, that none remained, or that they might not "visit" us again. This is why it's important to remember what happened with Megalithia. As a race, we have all but forgotten the aliens were ever here. That's not a good thing. To forget is never a good idea.

# PART 6
# THE FIRST GREAT DARK AGE
# AND
# RACIAL AMNESIA

# Chapter 18

## After the Fall of Megalithia

With the fall of Megalithia, the world was in a deplorable state. Virtually all population centers of any size whatsoever were gone. They were destroyed, or at least partially destroyed. Many coastal areas around the world had been inundated. Residual radiation, still existing in different areas, reveals thermonuclear weapons had been used, and certainly to a great effect. Starvation would have been a major problem for the remnants of humanity. What foodstuffs the war hadn't directly obliterated or poisoned with radiation, would have dwindled in the face of the onset of a nuclear winter. Moreover, with starvation comes pestilence.

The problems didn't end there. Megalithia was a top-down civilization. It had an over-structure, instead of an infrastructure. All political control and technology came from the aliens themselves. With the removal of all or at least most aliens (with perhaps the few remaining ones having very few capabilities left to them after the devastation of the war), the remnants of humanity had lost what little technology had been available to them.

It is doubtful they had the ability to recreate any of it. For instance, there is evidence humans might have flown vessels, the vimanas, for the aliens, but it isn't likely the aliens gave them the secrets of how to build such machinery. Since most transportation seems to have been done by air, using such devices, the loss of them would have instantly acted to isolate the remaining scattered and small fragment populations of humans. People were cut off. They were isolated.

Compounding this problem, with the flooding and submerging of all the coastal population centers, the only other means of transportation, shipping, (what little there may have been of it), was no longer available. Most of the ships in port would have gone along with the docking facilities. Even the methods and means of supplying such ships would have all been lost. Except for those few vessels that happened to be at sea at the time, all means of traveling by sea would have been lost to humanity.

All other forms of communication would have ceased as well, any electronic ones, certainly. Nuclear bombs give off powerful electromagnetic pulses (EMPs) that fry unshielded electronic equipment.

Since humanity had not yet domesticated horses, the only means of communication left was by walking on foot to their nearest neighbors. With the dangers that such travel would involve, after a series of nuclear blasts had left areas that were highly radioactive, along with roving bands of marauders, and perhaps even a few pockets of remaining aliens, it was unlikely much traveling, simply in order to maintain communications, would have been done.

However, there would have been those that traveled out of sheer necessity. They did this, if only to find food and shelter. These refugees would only have added to the general confusion and uncertainty of trying to maintain any lines of communication whatsoever.

To further exacerbate the problems, was the removal of the alien hierarchy, meaning the aliens themselves, along with their powerful human priesthood, and any puppet rulers they may have installed. This would have included members of their bureaucracy that would've been highly instrumental in handling the day-to-day affairs of most humans. Without the alien masters, ones whom humans may have had for thousands of years, humanity wouldn't have known what to do or where to turn to. All their lives and for countless generations, they had relied on these beings to tell them what to do. Suddenly, they were all gone.

This may be hard for us today to understand, to comprehend just how terrible it would have been for our ancestors. They had nothing left. They were severely reduced in numbers and had neither the technology nor the tools to create anything new. They had never been trained. They had never been taught how to do any of that. So what were they to do? They were alone, isolated, starving and diseased. Again, what were they to do?

Well they would do what any of us would do. They went on the move. We mentioned earlier in this book how the human population of the time was small to begin with, and many of them may still have been hunter-gatherers. The remaining urbanized humans had no choice, but to return to their old ways, too. Humans became hunters and gatherers again. City dwellers joined their rural cousins in this endeavor.

Humanity had entered the First Great Dark Age, as we call it. It was a far worse one than Europe endured after the fall of the Roman Empire. We became a retrograde culture, one where each successive generation couldn't do even what their immediate forebears could do. With the passing of time, we understood less and less. Little craftsmanship remained. The knowledge of how to do things was severely reduced. Only remnants of such knowledge remained, ones that might help in our day-to-day existence, our struggle to survive and find food.

The fact that more recent pottery shards dug from the ancient ruins of Mohenjo-Daro were less well created than the ones that came before them, is just one example of the evidence that supports this contention of ours. There are other examples. The fact is we were in a retrograde culture. With each passing generation, we lost more of what we had known before.

Just as when the Romans left England, and the natives then quickly forgot how to create concrete, and build the wondrous structures the Romans were capable of building, so too, did humanity forget how to build its megalithic monuments. With the end of the Megalithian Empire, the age of megalithic monuments was over at last.

As if overnight, all around the world, construction of such objects virtually ceased. The only exceptions were a few, isolated, and roughhewn copies that were still contrived to be built later by those wishing to emulate their former masters. Megalithia and its monuments vanished utterly. No one built the great platforms anymore, such as the ones at Baalbek and the Dome of the Rock.

Having gone through such a prolonged period, under such miserable circumstances the First Great Dark Age, is it any wonder we forgot about our alien masters and Megalithia? Is it any more unlikely, than the British people forgetting their overlords of several centuries, the Romans, within only a few generations of their departure?

The simple retreat of the Romans from Great Britain was enough to plunge the country into the dark ages and make them forget their masters had ever been there. Why should it be so difficult, then, to believe the same happened with the human race and their alien masters? Especially, when humanity endured such a traumatic removal of those who once controlled us, had undergone such extremes of destruction consequently?

With England, the Romans simply withdrew. They did not lay waste to the land. Yet, still they were quickly forgotten. With the aliens, there was war, destruction, starvation, and pestilence. They didn't just withdraw; the aliens, purposely or otherwise, had a scorched-earth policy carried out as they withdrew. Again, is it no wonder, after all that, we have forgotten they were ever here?

**Chapter Conclusion:** We have discussed here the fall of humanity as result of the collapse of Megalithia. That we became primitive and savage again, there is no doubt. How could we not under such circumstances? In addition, it was perhaps inevitable that we would lose almost all of our knowledge, whatever little the aliens had chosen to impart to us along the way. When you're grubbing for berries to feed your starving children in the forest, you are not too worried about how to create better pottery. The minimum amount of knowledge necessary for survival will do.

Nevertheless, one good thing did come out of all this for humanity. We were starting with a clean slate, almost entirely. Although it did take time, we began to regroup. Our numbers increased. Moreover, we're guessing that with what remnants of knowledge we still possessed from the Megalithian Empire, we were able, at least, to then eventually restart civilization.

This seems to have happened. Almost overnight, humanity regained civilization. Cities came into being again. Crafts developed. Knowledge of metallurgy advanced. Writing was invented. All the things we may have had once under the Megalithian overlords, we had again, but this time with a major difference. This time, we had accomplished it all for ourselves. Instead of an alien empire, we now had a very human one. Instead of having civilization created in the image of the aliens, civilization, at last, was created in our image.

Moreover, if our societies weren't perfect, if sometimes they closely resembled the governmental organization and tyranny, as well is dictatorship of the aliens, well then, that's to be expected. Racial memories of how we were once controlled may have lingered. For the sake of practicality, what worked for the aliens worked for humans, in many cases? Methods may often have been harsh, but they often were eminently practical. In any case, if our civilizations weren't perfect, just remember that neither was Megalithia, not by a long shot.

The future of human civilization may be uncertain. There were many obstacles in our past. There are many problems in our future to overcome if we are to survive as a species. Human civilization is fallible and there's no guarantee we will succeed in the long term.

However, for good or ill, for better or worse, there is one thing that can be said about our civilization. That is, it is human. This means it is our own, and so it is now up to us whether we succeed or fail. At least this way, the failures will be of our own making, and we can take pride in the successes as being entirely ours, as well.

However, this is only true if the aliens are well and truly

gone. However, what of the aliens? What happened to them? Where did they go? Are they still here in some capacity, however diminished? In our final chapter of Megalithia Ancient Alien Empire, we will attempt to come up with some answers to these questions.

# Chapter 19

## Where Are the Aliens Now?

**M**egalithia ended in a wave of devastation. But what of the aliens? What happened to them? Are they all gone? Did they flee the results of their own devastation and leave Earth and the Solar System alone, at long last? Did they all die? Or are they still here, just hidden from our view? And if so, why are they still here? What purpose would it serve for them now?

Many questions and the answers to them depend upon multiple factors. For instance, if traveling through interstellar space, was as easy for them as it is for us to hop in the car and go to the store, then it would be no problem for them all to leave and just go home. However, we have hints that even for them such travel to the stars wasn't very easy, or necessarily very quick, as in their capability to go faster than the speed of light.

Maybe they could, but we have historical clues that Einstein's theory of special relativity[215] still came into play. That is, those strange tricks of time that occur as one approaches the speed of light. Remember, if one is traveling almost at that speed onboard a spaceship, time appears perfectly normal to those onboard, but for the rest of the universe, from that crew's viewpoint, everything has actually speeded up.

For those not onboard the ship, they continue to grow older much faster compared to those onboard the ship. This process only occurs as one gets very close to the speed of light, but not when one passes it, if that is even possible. Many scientists say it is not.

We know the time dilation factor is real.[216] A number of experiments have been performed which invariably conclude that this is so. Even ships in orbit around the earth show a slight variance in the time aboard the ship compared to the time on Earth. From our vantage point on Earth, we see it as them lagging in time a little bit. It's just a tiny, minute fraction of a second, but it is enough to prove the theory of Einstein.

Therefore, if the aliens could not travel faster than the speed of light, we simply have to look for clues, some sort of evidence, and any sort that might prove this for us. There are no written records from this period, of course, but there are other stories, ancient ones, as from the Old Testament of the Bible, which would seem to indicate this time dilation effect did occur for certain people.

One of them was the Prophet Enoch, from the book of Enoch.[217] It was said he was taken up to heaven by "God," and taught many wonders by beings there. These beings actually had names. Then, he returned to earth to find that several generations had passed. Is this an example of the time dilation effect of traveling at speed of light?

One final note with regard to Enoch; supposedly, he didn't die. Rather, he was "translated" into heaven directly. In other words he ascended into "heaven," rather than dying on Earth. Perhaps, this is an early case of alien abduction being told here? There were other such ascensions into "heaven," as well. We already mentioned that Mohammed underwent this, and supposedly, so did Mary, the mother of Jesus, as well as others.

Moses, too, did something of a disappearing act. He went up to Mt. Sinai to receive the Ten Commandments. He was gone for forty days and forty nights. That's a long time! Either God was a very slow talker, and we mean no disrespect here, or a time dilation might have been involved. If Moses had been taken up by aliens and flown anywhere near the speed of light, it would've given him ample time to create the Ten Commandments. Of course, on Earth, more time would pass than onboard the ship. What might've been just a few days on the ship could have been forty days on Earth.

Another odd thing is how long Moses lived. In a time when lifespans were supposed to have been short, there are stories of him living to the incredible age of 800. However, the figure of 120 years is far more likely, because it is stated as such in Deuteronomy 34:7 as being so.

As the Bible states, Moses supposedly outlived all of his generation with but a couple of exceptions. Could time dilation have accounted for this, as well? When he was communing alone with God, was time (aboard an alien spacecraft?) going slower, while everyone on Earth was living at their normal rate. So were these little jaunts retarding his aging compared to those on Earth? Did Moses seem to go on living as others of his generation died of old age because of time dilation? When, in real time for him, he was just his own standard age? It's a possibility.

Again, there are more examples and intriguing hints about time dilation in the Bible and elsewhere, but we need to move on here. However, if this was so, this means the aliens either didn't have Faster-Than-Light (FTL) capability, or only some of them did. Those that did have it, probably decided to head for their home worlds. Those that didn't might have lingered here, some indefinitely. Alternatively, they might not have had a home world left to go to.

Therefore, in all likelihood, some if not many of the species of aliens did finally depart. But what about those that lingered? Where did they go? Are they still here?

It is possible some still are. After all, the aliens had a far superior technology to us, and probably had a greater ability of hanging onto it, if only in the form of the ships they traveled in. With time dilation as a factor, by traveling at speeds near that of light, many years, even centuries could pass on Earth, but just months for them. This would be another way of them increasing their longevity, without having to go too far from the vicinities of our solar system. They could have sped through the Big Freeze, for example, by doing this.

Moreover, there is other evidence of some of them still being here. William Bramley, as we've mentioned, makes some very convincing and in-depth arguments for some of them having remained. He points out that outside intervention seems to have been involved in many strange plagues that have stricken humanity, including the Black Death, which wiped out almost half the population of Europe in the Middle Ages.

He describes creatures cloaked and hooded, using objects that resembled scythes. These emitted noxious gases. Outbreaks of plague would occur in those regions within the next twenty-four hours. So often was this seen, so dominant did it become as an image in the human psyche of the times, that to this day, our images of death are of the skeleton cloaked and hooded, and wielding a scythe, reaping the lives of humans.

Bramley also cites numerous cases of strange lights seen in the sky, often before outbreaks of plague in any given area. He refers to witness testimony, of people often seeing strange greenish mists entering villages before the plague arrived. Again, his is an in-depth book, and one well worth reading.

However, William Bramley is not alone in arguing that aliens have been here throughout history. There are many other sources to help prove this point. For instance, there are the woodcuts of the famous aerial battle over Nuremberg, Germany, in the sixteenth century. There is another one of a similar battle over Basel, Switzerland.

Alexander the Great's contemporary historian spoke of silver flying shields maddening Alexander's war elephants, and striking terror into his soldiers. Since we've already discussed much of this earlier in this book, there is no need to recapitulate it all here. Suffice it to say this seems to be a great deal of evidence for aliens having been interfering in our lives for centuries upon centuries, and perhaps millennia.

What can we infer from this? Well, it would seem some of the aliens remained after the fall of Megalithia. What's more, it seems they were up to their same old tricks of trying to reduce the human population, if Bramley is correct. Strange plagues seem to have been and still may be one of their favorite methods. There certainly seems a good deal of evidence to support this idea.

Nevertheless, if they are here, where are they? Well, with the innumerable reports of USOs[218] (Unidentified Submerged Objects), and with many such reports coming from our own naval vessels, perhaps the aliens have taken refuge beneath the sea, or the bottom of large lakes.

There have been copious sightings of spacecraft or strange lights over lakes, bays, and even the ocean. Christopher Columbus, while approaching the New World, wrote of such lights in his log, and of them coming up out of the water. Perhaps the legends of Atlantis, an advanced civilization hiding beneath the ocean is actually referring to an alien base.

This last is just conjecture on our part, but there does seem to be a great many reports regarding UFOs in our skies, or USOs in our waters. They have been seen coming up out of our oceans and lakes, as well as diving into them. Reports of this have gone on for millennia. Therefore, we cannot rule out the possibility of alien bases as refuges beneath the seas.[219] Perhaps, our old masters are waiting there, lurking in the depths for a chance to challenge us for supremacy of the Earth once more.

Is it possible the aliens are hiding somewhere else, not on Earth,[220] but rather in the near vicinity of it? Certainly, with the type of spaceships they have, this would certainly seem feasible. But where should we look? Well, in our book, *DARKER SIDE OF THE MOON "They" Are Watching Us,* We point out that our nearest planetary neighbor, the moon, would be a great place for them to have secret bases. A report commissioned by NASA itself, NASA Technical Report R-277 Chronological Catalog of Reported Lunar Events (1968), which uses the best reputable sources to cite strange events on the moon, it refers to sightings of strange, transient, lunar events.

Using this report and the evidence contained in it, we feel

we have proved the point that something very weird has been going on there, on our satellite, and for a long time, perhaps for over 1,000 years or perhaps even thousands of years, or more!

Besides this, some people who worked for NASA, either directly, or as subcontractors, claim to have seen photographs of the ruins of alien bases on the moon. They claim NASA has airbrushed these out of photos released to the public. These people aren't fringe persons, but mainstream professionals with degrees, working for major corporations, often with excellent reputations, and so they have every right to be believed.[221]

Such people, as Milton Cooper, Naval Intelligence Officer, Maurice Chatelain, former Chief of NASA Communications Systems, and others, all claim that astronauts either photographed bases and/or ruins of bases on the moon, were shadowed by UFOs while visiting there, or even had near encounters with them. According to some, there were ancient mining operations on the moon and there are modern ones.[222] For more of an in-depth discussion on this, please check out DARKER SIDE OF THE MOON, "They" Are Watching Us!

So, if aliens could be beneath our oceans and lakes, and perhaps hiding on the moon in subterranean bases, as well, might they also be somewhere else in our solar system? The answer is, of course, yes. With their capabilities, that is not only a possibility, but perhaps even a distinct probability. Where is another likely place? Well, some say it might be on Titan, a moon of Saturn.[223] Maurice Chatelain claims that some UFOs could come from there.[224]

**Chapter Conclusion:** The end of Megalithia meant the end of the direct rule of the alien species. With the collapse of their control of the planet, and infrastructure on it, and their loss of control of the human race, many alien species probably simply decided to evacuate our solar system entirely, to go to their home worlds.

Other species may have been entirely wiped out in the course of the war. Certainly, all of them must have suffered losses, some more than others. Faced with a world in ruins, and the human population now free, though numbers severely reduced, those aliens who had to stay, for whatever reasons, had to adapt to the new situation.

The reasons for staying probably varied. Perhaps, as mentioned earlier, they stayed because their home worlds were destroyed. Alternatively, perhaps they stayed, because their species were subjugated by another alien species during the war. To return home was to return to slavery. For whatever reasons, some of them probably did stay behind. As shown above, we seem to have evidence to support this conclusion.

Moreover, some of the remnants of the remaining alien species probably decided to form coalitions in order to help survive. Others probably chose to go it alone. Regardless, none of them had the power to challenge humanity for supremacy of the Earth. They had neither the means, the wherewithal, nor probably even the desire after the collapse of Megalithia.

Their only other option was to stay in the vicinity, in hiding, as it were. Some may probably have adapted to this new existence, and preferred it this way. Maybe, if aliens are resident beneath our seas, they are perfectly happy to be there, and don't want much contact with us. They've learned to enjoy their solitude, perhaps.

Others may be actively interfering as best they can. With their technological capabilities, they probably influence our world more than we realize. However, compared to us, their numbers are not large, even now. That's almost a certainty, for we would certainly have run into them more often if they had large populations.

Therefore, although they probably still greatly surpass us, technologically speaking, their limited numbers do not allow them to seize outright control of our world once more. If we are still their slaves, it is in a way not readily apparent to us. That is a dark thought, that we are unwittingly being manipulated by them, genetically or otherwise. There is some evidence for this with the way they've interfered in our history, certainly.

However, if they couldn't control us when their numbers were greater and our population was much, much smaller, then we can hardly expect them to be able to control us now, with a human population exceeding seven billion on the planet. Good luck with that idea!

This does not mean that they still can't influence our world, perhaps even dictate to certain governments, and pose an ongoing and very real threat to our existence and hegemony of Earth. Are they still trying to make us over in their image? Some UFO conspiracy theorists believe this is so. They point to alien abductions of humans, and of alien breeding programs. Are we becoming them?

We simply don't know if this is true or not, but when it comes to aliens and UFOs; perhaps we should err always on the side of caution and not dismiss any idea out of hand. For that might be to our ultimate detriment.

# Conclusion

In this book, *Megalithia, Ancient Alien Empire*, we set out a bold series of statements at the beginning. We claimed there was an ancient alien empire that controlled the Earth long, before any human civilization was capable of doing so. We stated why we thought they were here, which was to pillage the earth of its resources. We even attempted to provide descriptions of the governmental structure of Megalithia, its type of architecture, its economy, social makeup, and its sciences and technologies.

Furthermore, we discussed these various aspects in detail. We attempted to provide evidence for all our contentions. As for the dating of the time of Megalithia, we made it clear that had to be somewhat fluid, because most dating processes of stone are somewhat inaccurate when it comes to when they were used to create structures.

Still, we do believe that Megalithia existed sometime before human civilization developed as we know it, and that it ended about 10,000 to 12,000 years ago. That, of necessity, has to be just an approximation, perhaps even a rough one. We feel by referring to the dating of various megalithic structures, the age of villages and cities that submerged, that we have made a good case for this time approximation.

Another of our contentions was that Megalithia collapsed due to interspecies or factional warfare amongst the alien rulers, as well as involving possible rebellions by humans. We cited the Vedas as evidence for this, referred to radioactive ruins, as well as radioactive skeletons, vitrified pottery, and vitrified forts. We believe these are all the products of a thermonuclear war, based on this evidence. We also feel there is a distinct possibility that asteroids were used as kinetic weapons, and that these, too, could result in climate change very similar to a nuclear winter, just as an atomic war would.

Another of our contentions is there was a major climate change to our planet as a result of that war, as well as a geographical change to the Earth's coastal regions. We have theorized The Younger Dryas "Big Freeze" was actually a nuclear winter. We also referred to the cultural legends of the Great Flood, as well as all the submerged cities around coastal regions of the world, to back up these contentions. We have even shown how it might have happened.

That the construction of megalithic structures around the world suddenly ceased, is a given. It is another of our contentions this shows that the civilization that could build them ceased to exist. Humanity was plunged into a First Great Dark Age, and it took millennia for us to come out of it, to begin to build civilization anew. This time, we would make it in our own way, in a human fashion, rather than an alien one.

We also contend that there still may be aliens around, either in hidden bases beneath the seas and lakes, or perhaps on our moon, or even on Titan. For all these contentions and more, we have given examples and several sorts of evidence. We've included many endnotes here, so that readers can research any given topic covered to a much greater degree, if they so choose. The sites these endnotes link to, also have links.

We did this because of necessity, we had to keep the examples, those items of possible evidence cited in the book, to a minimum here, or the book would have been simply too long and cumbersome. We feel it is up to each reader, individually, to arrive at their own conclusions based on the information we have given here, and whatever further research they wish to do on any particular topic by way of the included endnotes.

All these are just theories of ours, with regard to Megalithia,

The Younger Dryas, the destruction of the mega-fauna, a thermonuclear war, the cause of the Great Flood, and the aliens being here on our planet. However, we feel we have shown enough evidence at least to make a good case for our cause.

Again, it is up to each reader to decide for himself or herself if that case is strong enough. We reiterate here that we have included copious endnotes, so that readers may explore any of the subjects further for themselves. We just ask that they do it with an open mind.

One final note: we think Megalithia did exist. The standing stones, great platforms, and other stone structures that exist today are proof of that for us. We feel there is much other evidence to support this idea, as well. It is our belief that the First Great Dark Age, as we call it, the tremendous destruction that created those conditions, made us forget what came before. We feel this racial loss of memory definitely occurred. The human race has collective amnesia in this regard.

Perhaps we needed that after the traumas we suffered under the aliens and the Megalithian Empire. Nevertheless, today, more and more evidence is emerging that shows us something went before us, some civilization, and mother empire of empires, existed. We believe that was Megalithia, an alien-controlled civilization.

We also believe Megalithia; that first empire, was not for the benefit of humans. Oh, some of the alien species might have been relatively kind, might have wanted to help us, and in some ways did, but definitely, others did not.

Are they still lurking here today, the remnants of some of those species? We feel that very well might be the case. We also feel there is a tendency not to want to give up that collective amnesia with regard to our own history, that we're more comfortable this way. Nobody likes to have their boats rocked, and there is enough going on the world today without worrying about aliens. Right? At least, that seems to be the line of reasoning when we discuss these subjects with many others.

Even so, we think the aliens were here once, and may still be here now. Some may be friendly. Some most assuredly still are our foes. That, we feel, is worth considering, at the very least.

There is an old saying, "Those who forget history are condemned to repeat it." Is this a tired old cliché? You bet it is! However, it has hung around for a very long time now and there is a reason for that, even though it is such a cliché. You see, it's also very true.

When it comes to our collective amnesia with regard to Ancient Alien Empire, Megalithia, we would do well to remember that. If we don't, we might just end up by becoming a subjugated people once more.

# ABOUT THE AUTHORS

Rob Shelsky is an avid and eclectic writer, and averages about 4,000 words a day. Rob, with a degree in science, has written a large number of factual articles for the former AlienSkin Magazine, as well as for other magazines, such as Doorways, Midnight Street (U.K.), Internet Review of Science Fiction (IROSF), and many others. While at AlienSkin Magazine, a resident columnist there for about seven years, Rob did a number of investigative articles, including some concerning the paranormal, as well as columns about UFOs, including interviews of those who have had encounters with them.

Along with the late George Kempland, both authors have often and over a long period, explored the Alien and UFO question together. They've made investigative trips to research such UFO hotspot areas as Pine Bush, New York, Gulf Breeze, Florida, and other such regions, including Brown Mountain, North Carolina, known, for the infamous "Brown Mountain Lights, as well as investigating numerous places known for paranormal activity.

With over 20 years of such research and investigative efforts behind them, Authors George Kempland and Rob Shelsky are well qualified in the subject of UFOs, as well as that of the paranormal. Where Rob Shelsky tends to be the skeptic, and insists upon being able to "kick the tires" of a UFO, to ascertain their reality, George Kempland is the theorist, constantly coming up with possible explanations for various such phenomena. Together, they make a powerful investigative team when it comes to tackling the hard questions about UFOs and what they might mean for us all.

For links to other books written, please go to:

http://home.earthlink.net/~robngeorge/

Or: http://robshelsky.blogspot.com/

Or:

http://www.amazon.com/gp/search/ref=sr_tc_2_0?rh=i%3Ast
rip-
books%2Ck%3ARob+Shelsky&keywords=Rob+Shelsky&ie=U
TF8&qid=1298820526&sr=1-2-ent&field-
contributor_id=B002BO9RIE

# Endnotes

[1] http://en.wikipedia.org/wiki/Accelerating_change

[2] http://www-rohan.sdsu.edu/faculty/vinge/misc/singularity.html

[3] http://www.turing.org.uk/scrapbook/test.html

[4] http://en.wikipedia.org/wiki/Transhumanism

[5] http://www.mooreslaw.org/

[6] http://www.kurzweilai.net/kurzweils-law-aka-the-law-of-accelerating-returns

[7] http://thenextweb.com/insider/2011/06/19/what-is-the-technological-singularity/

[8] http://en.wikipedia.org/wiki/Ray_Kurzweil

[9] http://en.wikipedia.org/wiki/Accelerating_change#Vinge.27s_exponentially_accelerating_change

[10] http://www.universetoday.com/13741/the-odds-of-intelligent-life-in-the-universe/

[11] http://moonphases.info/number-of-stars-in-the-milky-way.html

[12] http://www.extremetech.com/extreme/152573-astronomers-estimate-100-billion-habitable-earth-like-planets-in-the-milky-way-50-sextillion-in-the-universe

[13] http://www2.astro.psu.edu/users/dfox/A001/Notes/lec37.html

[14] http://www.cfa.harvard.edu/news/2012/pr201219.html

[15] http://www.slate.com/blogs/bad_astronomy/2013/03/21/age_of_the_universe_planck_results_show_universe_is_13_82_billion_years.html

[16] http://abyss.uoregon.edu/~js/cosmo/lectures/lec28.html

[17] http://www.vaughns-1-pagers.com/history/world-population-growth.htm#population-growth-chart

[18] http://www.painofsalvation.com/be/population.htm

[19] http://www.getbig.com/boards/index.php?topic=354457.0

[20] http://en.wikipedia.org/wiki/Younger_Dryas

[21] http://en.wikipedia.org/wiki/Mining_in_Roman_Britain

[22] http://en.wikipedia.org/wiki/Roman_roads_in_Britain

[23] http://en.wikipedia.org/wiki/End_of_Roman_rule_in_Britain

[24] http://en.wikipedia.org/wiki/Baalbek

[25] http://www.sitchin.com/landplace.htm

[26] http://atheism.about.com/od/religiousplaces/ig/Baalbek-Temples-Lebanon/Baalbek-Trilithon-Stone-Blocks.htm

[27] http://secrettruthrevealed.blogspot.com/2009/09/giants-built-temples-of-baalbek-in.html

[28] http://en.wikipedia.org/wiki/10th_millennium_BC

[29] http://extraterrestrialcontact.com/tag/baalbek/

[30] http://www.sitchin.com/

[31] http://christianity.about.com/od/Old-Testament/a/JZ-Sacrifice-Of-Isaac.htm

[32] http://en.wikipedia.org/wiki/Holy_of_Holies

[33] http://www.spiritofmaat.com/archive/nov2/sitchin.htm

[34] http://askville.amazon.com/Temple-Solomon-temple%27s-importance-Judaism-Christianity/AnswerViewer.do?requestId=4274900

[35] http://www.paranormalhaze.com/72-demons-evoked-by-king-solomon/

[36]http://www.ancient.eu.com/eridu/

[37] http://www.bibliotecapleyades.net/sumer_anunnaki/godsnewmillemnium/godsnewmillemnium08.htm

[38] http://proteus.brown.edu/mesopotamianarchaeology/477

[39] http://www.ancient.eu.com/eridu/

[40] http://www.biblegateway.com/passage/?search=Genesis+11%3A1-9&version=NIV

[41] http://abcnews.go.com/Technology/evidence-suggests-biblical-great-flood-noahs-time-happened/story?id=17884533

[42] http://ngm.nationalgeographic.com/2010/03/nasca/hall-text

[43] http://www.toplessrobot.com/2011/08/6_ancient_things_that_were_probably_built_by_alien.php

[44] https://www.google.com/search?q=arizona+mesas&ie=utf-8&oe=utf-8&aq=t&rls=org.mozilla:en-US:official&client=firefox-a

[45] http://www.change.freeuk.com/learning/relthink/nightjourney.html

[46] http://www.jewishvirtuallibrary.org/jsource/Judaism/ark.html

[47] http://www.davidicke.com/forum/showthread.php?t=219647

[48] http://www.world-mysteries.com/mpl_5b5.htm

[49] http://paranormal.about.com/od/demonsandexorcism/a/aa060506.htm

[50] http://www.chabad.org/library/article_cdo/aid/112333/jewish/Nimrod-and-Abraham.htm

[51] http://classiclit.about.com/library/bl-etexts/lginzberg/bl-lginzberg-legends-1-5f.htm

[52] http://en.wikipedia.org/wiki/G%C3%B6bekli_Tepe

[53] http://en.wikipedia.org/wiki/Last_glacial_period

[54] http://classiclit.about.com/library/bl-etexts/lginzberg/bl-lginzberg-legends-1-5f.htm

[55] http://www.bradshawfoundation.com/lascaux/

[56] http://beforeitsnews.com/beyond-science/2013/01/25000-year-old-buildings-found-in-russia-the-mysterious-dolmens-and-megaliths-of-the-caucasus-2440682.html

[57] http://en.wikipedia.org/wiki/Dolmens_of_North_Caucasus

[58] http://www.megalithomania.co.uk/hughnewman.html

[59] http://blog.world-mysteries.com/science/the-alignments-of-carnac/

[60] http://thewarriormuse.blogspot.com/2013/04/c-is-for-carnac-stones-plus-mww-iwsg.html

[61] http://www.philipcoppens.com/carnac.html

[62] http://books.google.com/books?id=Zl356ACEhs0C&pg=PA163&lpg=PA163&dq=Stones+of+Carnac+and+ley+lines&source=bl&ots=yqNIe413kC&sig=cKfnCoLWJLVB4GwZ9GVrhA_0EJs&hl=en&sa=X&ei=blc_UqmpDa--4APY54CQCQ&ved=0CDUQ6AEwAQ#v=onepage&q=Stones%20of%20Carnac%20and%20ley%20lines&f=false

[63] http://beforeitsnews.com/beyond-science/2013/08/indonesian-pyramid-is-20000-years-old-claims-archaeologist-discovery-may-rewrite-history-2442948.html

[64] http://www.abovetopsecret.com/forum/thread880575/pg1

[65] http://www.viewzone.com/tiax.html

[66] http://talc.site88.net/mega.htm

[67] http://www.crystalinks.com/egyptnews.html

[68] https://www.google.com/search?q=Puma+Punku&ie=utf-8&oe=utf-8&aq=t&rls=org.mozilla:en-US:official&client=firefox-a

[69] http://en.wikipedia.org/wiki/Yonaguni_Monument

[70] http://www.robertschoch.com/sphinxcontent.html

[71] http://www.robertschoch.com/geodatasphinx.html

[72] http://anthropology.msu.edu/anp264-ss13/2013/02/07/aliens-and-the-pyramids-of-giza-2/

[73] http://jcolavito.tripod.com/lostcivilizations/id10.html

[74] http://www.angelfire.com/jazz/louxsie/pyramidrant.html

[75] http://www.gizapyramid.com/stephen%20mehler%20research%20article.htm

[76] http://news.discovery.com/history/ancient-egypt/pyramids-hieroglyphs-robot-mystery-110526.htm

[77] http://robertbauval.co.uk/articles/articles/scsequel2.html

[78] http://www.ancientegyptonline.co.uk/kingschambergp.html

[79] http://www.bibliotecapleyades.net/piramides/esp_piramide_8.htm#The%20Orion%20Mystery

[80] http://doernenburg.alien.de/alternativ/orion/ori00_e.php

[81] http://blog.world-mysteries.com/mystic-places/ancient-cities-and-megalithic-sites-underwater/

[82] http://eden-saga.com/en/atlantide-ys-nazado-halieis-tartessos-dorestad-vineta-scilly-dunwich-villes-englouties.html

[83] http://www.bagadoo.tm.fr/kemper/villedys_e.html

[84] http://ancienthistory.about.com/od/lostcontinent/qt/072507Atlantis.htm

[85] http://www.decadevolcano.net/santorini/atlantis.htm

[86] http://voyagesextraordinaires.blogspot.com/2009/03/lost-land-of-lyonesse.html

[87] http://www.metoperafamily.org/metopera/history/stories/synopsis.aspx?customid=86

[88] http://www.huffingtonpost.com/dr-jon-c-henderson/pavlopetri_b_1568039.html

[89] http://www.antiquities.org.il/article_Item_eng.asp?sec_id=14&subj_id=139

[90] http://www.grahamhancock.com/news/index.php?search=mahabalipuram

[91] http://www.archaeologyonline.net/artifacts/cambay.html

[92] http://en.wikipedia.org/wiki/Lemuria_%28continent%29

[93] http://en.wikipedia.org/wiki/Mu_%28lost_continent%29

[94] https://www.forbiddenhistory.info/?q=node/72

[95] http://www.agoracosmopolitan.com/news/headline_news/2012/10/07/4547.html

[96] http://truththeory.com/2012/05/15/most-dinosaur-bones-discovered-are-radioactive/

[97] http://en.wikipedia.org/wiki/Isotopes_of_iridium

[98] http://www.businessinsider.com/how-humans-and-dinosaurs-coexisted-2013-4

[99] http://www.bible.ca/tracks/tracks-cambodia.htm

[100] http://www.bible.ca/tracks/peru-tomb-art.htm

[101] http://www.ufoevidence.org/documents/doc1249.htm

[102] http://www.icr.org/article/amazing-anomalous-fossil/

[103] http://en.wikipedia.org/wiki/Thomas_Robert_Malthus

[104] http://en.wikipedia.org/wiki/Malthusianism

[105] http://en.wikipedia.org/wiki/Zecharia_Sitchin

[106] http://www.openbible.info/topics/nephilim

[107] http://library.thinkquest.org/5830/DemiGods.htm

[108] http://www.mtpioneer.com/2013-February-Legends-of-the-Star-People.html

[109] https://en.wikipedia.org/wiki/Elohim

[110] http://ksuweb.kennesaw.edu/~shagin/060818mesopchars.pdf

[111] http://www.shamanicjourneys.com/articles/glossaryofthegods.php

[112] http://www.bibliotecapleyades.net/sumer_anunnaki/anunnaki/anu_22.htm

[113] http://www.godlikeproductions.com/forum1/message1888098/pg1

[114] http://en.wikipedia.org/wiki/Quetzalcoatl

[115] https://www.google.com/search?q=Annunaki+had+wings?&client=firefox-a&hs=Jwx&rls=org.mozilla:en-US:official&tbm=isch&tbo=u&source=univ&sa=X&ei=2vPOUcDPCJG-9QSXi4HwCg&ved=0CC0QsAQ&biw=1024&bih=610

[116] http://www.gatewaystobabylon.com/myths/texts/enki/enkieridu.htm

[117] http://en.wikipedia.org/wiki/Abzu

[118] http://www.viewzone.com/adamscalendar.html
http://www.viewzone.com/adamscalendar.html

[119] http://www.youtube.com/watch?v=ZyWplRoVAcc

[120] http://en.wikipedia.org/wiki/Machadodorp

[121] http://subharanjangupta.wordpress.com/2011/08/01/earth-energy-grid-portals-and-other-mysterious-places-2/

[122] http://hiddenarchaeology.com/2011/06/354/ancient-mines-on-earth/

[123] http://blog.world-mysteries.com/strange-artifacts/unexplained-band-of-holes-pisco-peru/

[124] http://cassiopaea.org/forum/index.php?topic=17629.0

[125] http://bruhaspati.com/technology/ancient-technology/springs-screws-and-metals-from-russia.html

[126] http://www.etdaily.com/categories/alien/item/1179-russian-scientists-prove-dashka-stone-map-of-the-creator-is-real

[127] http://english.pravda.ru/news/russia/30-04-2002/42113-0/

[128] http://www.livinginthelightms.com/shambhalaufos

[129] http://www.veda.harekrsna.cz/encyclopedia/warhistory.htm

[130] http://en.wikipedia.org/wiki/Ramayana

[131] http://larryavisbrown.homestead.com/files/xeno.mahabsynop.htm

[132] http://www.viking-mythology.com/ragnarok.html

[133] http://www.godlikeproductions.com/forum1/message744236/pg1

[134] http://en.wikipedia.org/wiki/Dogon_people

[135] http://www.abovetopsecret.com/forum/thread394155/pg1

[136] http://en.wikipedia.org/wiki/Artificial_cranial_deformation

[137] http://www.dailymail.co.uk/sciencetech/article-2250145/The-incredible-alien-skull-discovered-Mexican-cemetery.html

[138] http://beforeitsnews.com/alternative/2012/12/elongated-alien-skulls-found-in-mexico-2525886.html

[139] https://en.wikipedia.org/wiki/Artificial_cranial_deformation

[140] http://www.starchildproject.com/dna2012.htm

[141] http://www.starchildproject.com/

[142] http://en.wikipedia.org/wiki/Akhenaten

[143] http://en.wikipedia.org/wiki/Ancient_Egyptian_deities

[144] http://en.wikipedia.org/wiki/Elongated_human_skulls

[145] http://hiddenincatours.com/elongated-skulls-of-paracas-a-people-and-their-world/

[146] http://weeklyworldnews.com/aliens/6638/elongated-skulls-discovered/

[147] http://thegreaterpicture.com/skulls.html

[148] https://www.google.com/search?q=aliens+and+elongated+skulls&client=firefox-a&hs=vxQ&rls=org.mozilla:en-US:official&tbm=isch&tbo=u&source=univ&sa=X&ei=XKeoUab5BtKC0QGP7YD4Bg&ved=0CDcQsAQ&biw=1012&bih=566

[149] http://io9.com/5967785/new-interpretation-of-extinct-hobbit-species-reveals-a-human+like-face

[150] http://www.davidicke.com/forum/archive/index.php/t-8506.html

[151] http://en.wikipedia.org/wiki/Kukulkan

[152] http://www.abovetopsecret.com/forum/thread459147/pg1

that are so specific, so heavily detailed

[153] http://www.amazon.com/dp/0380718073/?tag=mh0b-20&hvadid=166982521&ref=pd_sl_5aoa3stzex_e

[154] http://en.wikipedia.org/wiki/Alcubierre_drive

[155] http://www.geekation.com/a-planetary-defense-system-set-up-for-us-by-aliens-hundreds-of-years-ago/

[156] http://www.realufos.net/2011/10/close-look-at-valley-of-death-yakutian.html

[157] http://beforeitsnews.com/paranormal/2012/07/scientists-find-further-proof-of-ancient-alien-technology-2364829.html

[158] http://www.politicsforum.org/forum/viewtopic.php?f=50&t=149183

[159] http://theyreal.com/the-mystery-of-puma-punku-ancient-miracles-or-alien-technology/

[160] http://carrollbryant.blogspot.com/2012/09/ufo-files-peruvian-stargate.html

[161] http://www.abovetopsecret.com/forum/thread160231/pg1

[162] http://www.thelivingmoon.com/42stargate/03files/Sumerian_Gate.html

[163] https://www.google.com/search?q=Pyramid+of+giza+as+a+power+plant&client=firefox-a&hs=Qx3&rls=org.mozilla:en-US:official&tbm=isch&tbo=u&source=univ&sa=X&ei=BwEBUryrLIPm9ASt3YDwDQ&ved=0CD0QsAQ&biw=1024&bih=600

[164] http://www.gizapower.com/

[165] http://www.gizapower.com/Model2.htm

[166] http://www.ufodigest.com/article/ancient-aliens-and-ark-covenant

[167] http://beforeitsnews.com/paranormal/2010/09/ancient-aliens-and-the-ark-of-the-covenant-by-paul-schroeder-158206.html

[168] http://www.ancient-code.com/ancient-technology/

[169] http://www.forteantimes.com/features/articles/256/sonic_weapons.html

[170] http://ufo.whipnet.org/xdocs/alexander.the.great/

[171] http://mysteryufosaliens.webs.com/aliensancientpictures.htm

[172] http://coolinterestingstuff.com/the-madonna-with-saint-giovannino-ufo-painting

[173] Aert De Gelder

[174] http://www.sanandaseagles.com/pages/spacecraft_in_art.html

[175] http://www.nationalgallery.org.uk/paintings/carlo-crivelli-the-annunciation-with-saint-emidius

[176] http://unmyst3.blogspot.com/2011/04/mysterious-painting-of-bonaventura.html

[177] http://www.aquiziam.com/ancient-technology.html

[178] http://www.google.com/imgres?imgurl=http://www.bibliotecapleyades.net/egipto/imagenes/abydos02.jpg&imgrefurl=http://www.bibliotecapleyades.net/egipto/esp_abydos03.htm&h=886&w=1240&sz=204&tbnid=NSZNfYDU9eUMaM:&tbnh=100&tbnw=140&zoom=1&usg=__ri_aUP-34S5sYlNKhK-6qdA23dA=&docid=QWOSJm_FXIfhBM&sa=X&ei=PegEUrO0EJP84AP2k4HIBw&ved=0CFIQ9QEwBQ&dur=410

[179] http://www.thelivingmoon.com/43ancients/02files/Ancient_Electricity_02.html

[180] http://www.discoveringegypt.com/Dendera1.htm

[181] http://www.unmuseum.org/bbattery.htm

[182] http://www.bibliotecapleyades.net/vimanas/esp_vimanas_2a.htm

[183] http://www.ufoevidence.org/documents/doc173.htm

[184] http://www.realistnews.net/Thread-5000-year-old-ufo-vimana-discovered-in-afghanistan-c2c-with-stephen-quayle

[185] http://ufo.whipnet.org/creation/ancient.aircraft/vimanas.html
[186] http://www.ece.lsu.edu/kak/MahabharataII.pdf
[187] http://www.crystalinks.com/vimanas.html
[188]

http://www.bibliotecapleyades.net/ciencia/antigravityworldgrid/cienci
a_antigravityworldgrid01.htm
[189] http://www.youtube.com/watch?v=a6rQ9dfoxZM
[190]

https://www.google.com/search?q=images+of+ancient+aliens&client
=firefox-a&hs=roV&rls=org.mozilla:en-
US:official&tbm=isch&tbo=u&source=univ&sa=X&ei=natBUpe6Fs
6i4APbiYDYDQ&ved=0CCwQsAQ&biw=1024&bih=583&dpr=1
[191]

https://www.google.com/search?q=ancient+sumerian+gods&client=fi
refox-a&hs=Pge&rls=org.mozilla:en-
US:official&tbm=isch&tbo=u&source=univ&sa=X&ei=lRE2Us_OH
5W14AOKvYCYAg&ved=0CDgQsAQ&biw=1024&bih=610&dpr=
1
[192]

http://www.bibliotecapleyades.net/sociopolitica/sociopol_brotherhoo
dsnake05.htm
[193] http://en.wikipedia.org/wiki/Serpent_Mound
[194] http://www.seancasteel.com/angels_and_aliens.htm
[195] http://www.xfacts.com/eyes.htm
[196] http://www.ancient-code.com/temehea-tohua-an-alien-race-
depicted/
[197] http://en.wikipedia.org/wiki/Anthropomorphism
[198] http://faculty.gvsu.edu/websterm/Gods&men.htm
[199]

http://www.bibliotecapleyades.net/vida_alien/alien_races03.htm
[200] http://www.armaghplanet.com/blog/the-truth-about-zeta-
reticuli.html
[201] http://www.ufoevidence.org/topics/dogon.htm
[202] http://www.ufocasebook.com/Hill.html
[203]

http://en.wikipedia.org/wiki/Betty_and_Barney_Hill_abduction
[204] http://mattovermatter.com/2010/10/alien-genetics-found-
interbred-with-human-dna/
[205] http://www.beforeus.com/indusa.htm

206

http://www.bibliotecapleyades.net/vimanas/esp_vimanas_3.htm

207

http://www.bibliotecapleyades.net/ancientatomicwar/esp_ancient_ato
mic_07.htm

208

http://www.bibliotecapleyades.net/vimanas/esp_vimanas_3.htm

209 https://www.forbiddenhistory.info/?q=node/130

210 a small regional nuclear war could create our worst night-
mare, a nuclear winter lasting about 10 years (!).

211

http://www.scientificamerican.com/article.cfm?id=megafauna-
extinction-affects-ecosystems-12000-years-later

212

http://www.dnr.state.mn.us/young_naturalists/pleistocene_megafauna
.html

213 http://www.livescience.com/10203-66-foot-waves-hit-york-
ancient-asteroid-splashdown.html

214 http://en.wikipedia.org/wiki/Younger_Dryas

215 http://www.dummies.com/how-to/content/einsteins-special-
relativity.html

216 http://en.wikipedia.org/wiki/Time_dilation

217

http://en.wikipedia.org/wiki/Enoch_%28ancestor_of_Noah%29

218 http://www.mysterypile.com/uso.php

219 http://ufos.about.com/od/ufohistory/a/usos.htm

220 http://reinep.wordpress.com/2011/02/27/nasas-secrets-
revealed-alien-ruins-on-the-moon/

221 http://www.helpfreetheearth.com/news87_moon.html

222 http://ufodigest.com/article/alien-bases-moon

223 http://www.liveleak.com/view?i=6fb_1375017589

224

http://www.bibliotecapleyades.net/ciencia/supressed_inventions/supp
ressed_inventions31.htm

Made in the USA
Lexington, KY
06 January 2015